Typhoon
and Tempest
at War

Typhoon and Tempest

at War

Arthur Reed
Roland Beamont

LONDON
IAN ALLAN LTD

First published 1974

ISBN 0 7110 0542 7

Published by Ian Allan Ltd, Shepperton, Surrey
and printed in the United Kingdom by
Ian Allan (Printing) Ltd.

Contents

The Genius of Sydney Camm

Sir Sydney Camm, 'father' of the Typhoon – Tempest series of aircraft. This brilliant designer had been in charge at Hawker's Kingston-upon-Thames works for 12 years when discussions on the series started in 1937, and during that time he had produced a stream of successful military aeroplanes, including the Hart, the Fury and the Hurricane. A warm and generous man who cloaked these qualities with a brusque exterior, he drove his colleagues hard in the search for perfection. He was knighted in 1953, and died March 12, 1966.

Behind the Typhoon and the Tempest lay the genius of one man, Sydney Camm. This brilliant aircraft designer had already been in charge of the drawing office at the Kingston-upon-Thames, Surrey, works of Hawker for 12 years when discussions about this project that was to become the Typhoon started in 1937. He had fathered a stream of successful military aeroplanes, including the Hart and the Fury and, above all, the Hurricane, during that time.

Knighted in 1953, Sir Sydney died in 1966. He is remembered by his contemporaries as a warm and generous man who cloaked these qualities with a brusque exterior. During the period of the early development of the Typhoon, as the inevitability of World War II became apparent, and the pace and pressures of the national rearmament programme quickened, the design team at Kingston was spurred on mercilessly by Camm in his search for perfection.

One of those with clear impressions remaining of those hectic days is Mr Robert Lickley, now assistant managing director, Hawker Siddeley Aviation, in the modern Kingston works. He said, 'We were able to get a few of our own ideas into the design, but nothing went through on the Tornado — Typhoon programme that he did not personally approve.

'He would deal with even quite small items, and all the discussions and the arguments and the master — minding with the Ministry on specifications, and whether it should have eight or 12 guns, he handled himself.

'In spite of having two different engines in the otherwise similar Tornado and Typhoon, and major changes in design, we did this aeroplane in two years. We were under constant and heavy pressure from Sir Sydney, who never let up. He had no other interests at the time but his aeroplanes, and he just pushed and pushed, and all of us worked at the same rate.

'At the same time as we were designing the Typhoon, we were also working on developments of the Hart and the Hurricane, but we were only 100 people in the design office. There was no time to

do anything else but your damndest — and get it right first time.

'Most of us were working the normal 42½ hour week, plus three nights overtime, and Sunday mornings as well. Camm had a one-track mind — his aircraft were right, and everybody had to work on them to get them right. If they did not, then there was hell.

'He was a very brilliant chief designer. He was a very difficult man to work for, but you could not have a better aeronautical engineer to work under. You would be at your desk first thing in the morning, hoping for half an hour to clear things up, when you would get a buzz from Camm, who wanted to start where you had left off the previous evening.

'It was obvious that he has been giving the problem a lot of thought during the night. He was very kind and considerate to everybody if they were not connected with the aeroplane on the go at that time. More than any other chief designer at that time, he had a tremendous feeling for the risks that the test pilots took. He would never ask them to risk their lives if he could help it.'

Mr Lickley took the Sydney Camm story further in a lecture which he presented in 1971 at the Royal Aeronautical Society. 'His methods with the user varied, but visits invariably started with a battle, unless the visitor was one of those for whom Camm had real respect. Those who survived these slanging matches, however, found that their views were respected and accepted, and before their next visit were likely to be incorporated in the design.

'With regard to his own staff, he did not suffer fools gladly, and at times many of us appeared to be fools. One rarely got into trouble for doing something either in the ideas line, or in the manufacturing line, but woe betide those who did nothing, or who put forward an indeterminate solution.'

'Plagued in the early days by engine problems, and having elevator flutter problems which caused failure of the rear fuselage, the Typhoon had an unhappy start; but by the time of the invasion of Normandy its striking power in low-level operations was of tremendous advantage in dealing with enemy ground forces. In this work, 1,000lb bombs, or eight 3in rockets were carried under the wings.

'While the Typhoon was still in teething troubles, discussions were taking place with the Director of Technical Development for its successor. The lessons learned from the Typhoon were incorporated — wing thickness was reduced from 18 percent to 14½ percent longer range was provided, and the Bristol Centaurus radial engine was considered, as well as the latest Sabre.

'The design was successful, and went ahead as the Tempest V (Sabre) and Tempest II (Centaurus). The Tempest V, built at Kingston and Langley, went into service in 1944 and performed outstanding service against the flying bombs, but the Tempest II, built by Bristol at Weston-super-Mare, was only just going into service when the war ended.

'Again, the ability of a Camm design to handle successfully more than one type of engine was shown, and Tempest IIs were also supplied to India and Pakistan after World War II."

'Still striving after higher performance and before the Tempest became operational, discussions took place between Camm and the Air Ministry for a Tempest light fighter. This was a Tempest with a reduced wing area, a Centaurus engine, and a considerably improved view for the pilot. Before long it was named Fury, and a Sea Fury version was also started.

'The Sea Fury was another success story, going into service with the Royal Navy in 1946, seeing service in the Korean war, and remaining in service until 1953, when replaced by the Sea Hawk. With the Sea Fury, the second stream (of aircraft design) came to an end. In its development the ultimate in design of fighter aircraft using piston engines had been reached. A series which

started with the feeling that four .303 guns were the biggest load a wing could take, ended with loads in service reaching 1,500lb per wing.

'With the exception of the flutter trouble on the early Typhoon, none of these aircraft suffered from structural failure, and all through World War II showed a capability to take heavy punishment and return safely to base. This record was not achieved at the expense of performance, because the structure weight percentages were low by then-prevailing standards, but by careful attention to detail design and choice of materials.'

Camm's remarkable career, from his birth, at Windsor, in 1893, to his death in 1966, spanned a brief era in which aviation had accelerated from man-lifting kites to Concorde, from balloons to ballistic rockets and preparations to land men on the moon. In 1912 he and fellow members of the Windsor Model Aeroplane Club were engaged on the design and manufacture of a man-carrying glider. A few months before his death, Camm was in correspondence with engine manufacturers about the potential of a fighter to fly at four times the speed of sound.

In between came the highly successful Hunter jet fighter, the P.1127 prototype of the Harrier, the world's first operational vertical take-off and landing fighter, and the Typhoon-Tempest series, the deployment of which gave an undoubted impetus towards victory by the Allies in World War II.

To all these projects, Camm applied a simple philosophy — see the need, and set out to provide for it; work closely with the engine company to ensure the best possible marriage of engine and airframe; keep things as simple as possible, both in layout and construction; and do not go too far beyond the existing states of knowledge in too many areas at once.

Camm's fascination with aeroplanes was apparent at an early age as shown by this picture of him with a model, taken at Byfleet, Surrey, in 1915 when he was aged 18. A few years earlier he had been a founder member of the Windsor Model Aeroplane Club which, in 1912, designed and flew a man-carrying glider. Camm cycled regularly at weekends to Brooklands to study the rudimentary aircraft there, and would make acid reports back to his fellow club members. 'Struts like floorboards', he commented on one machine.

A Clash of Arms

Highly appropriately, final completion of the first Typhoon took place on the day World War II was declared, Sunday, September 3, 1939. Hawker workers who were there on that dramatic day recall struggling back towards London from the vast new factory at Langley, Buckinghamshire, in the face of traffic carrying people trying to leave the capital.

Early design work had started in 1936, with Air Ministry specification F.18/37 being written around Hawker ideas of late 1936 — early 1937. This called for the production of two new interceptor fighters to succeed the Hurricane and the Spitfire, with a speed increment of at least 100mph, and with much heavier armament. Thinking in the Air Council at that time was strongly in favour of providing the RAF with intense fire-power. Their proposal was for the new fighters to be armed with four 20mm cannon, so producing a clash with Hawker's ideas which ran more along the lines of twelve .303in machine-guns.

An example of the farsightedness of Camm is provided by the fact that he had been closely studying the design for the aircraft which eventually became the short-lived predecessor of the Typhoon, the Tornado, for seven months before the first flight of *its* predecessor, the first production model of the Hurricane Mark 1, on October 12, 1937.

Appendix B of the F.18/37 specification, containing the operational requirement for the new aircraft in detail, was sent out to ten manufacturing companies on January 15, 1938. With the exception of the divergence of views over exactly what the armament should be, the design work that Hawker, under the guidance of Camm, had already done and the Air Council's plans fitted hand-in-glove.

There was no surprise in the industry when Hawker's tenders were accepted on April 22, 1938. Orders for the commencement of prototypes had in fact already been given by that time by the management of the company.

Four prototypes were ordered by the Air Ministry, the instruction being that two should be fitted with the Napier

Left: First of the family. The first prototype Tornado made its maiden flight with Philip Lucas at the controls on October 6, 1939, had a Rolls-Royce Vulture 24-cylinder liquid-cooled engine and its radiator scoop positioned between the wings in a similar position to that on the Hurricane. But this placing caused buffeting at high speeds, and it was soon moved forward to become the big chin radiator so characteristic of the Typhoon and the Tempest V and VI.

Below: An historic photograph showing the scene at the Hawkers airfield at Langley on the day, February 24, 1940, that the first Typhoon prototype made its maiden flight, with Philip Lucas at the controls. He recalled that the first flight lasted 30 minutes, after there had been some doubt whether it should be made at all at that time, due to the fact that the wind was blowing in the wrong direction.

The rear of the early radiator position on the prototype Tornado seen in close-up in the two accompanying pictures.

Sabre, a 24-cylinder engine with four rows of six cylinders arranged in an 'H' layout, driving two crankshafts. The other two were to use the Rolls-Royce Vulture, comprising two 12-cylinder engines joined in an 'X' layout, driving a common crankshaft. The third engine in the market, the Bristol Centaurus, was not proceeded with at that time because it was not considered to be far enough advanced. Later versions of it powered the successful Tempest II.

This range of, for those days, enormously powerful new engines in the 2,000hp bracket had been pioneered by the engine companies themselves, with little assistance or encouragement from the government. Working closely with the airframe firms, the engine manufacturers had anticipated the trend towards bigger and more powerful successors for the Hurricanes and the Spitfires. But such was the leap forward, and such the pressure under which they were being asked to work, it was hardly surprising that major problems arose — problems which were to shake to the foundations, and almost sink, the whole Typhoon project.

From Hawker's point of view, there were few technical problems in adapting their airframe to take either Sabres or Vultures. The two versions were designated the N-type, for the Napier Sabre (the Typhoon) and the R-type, for the Rolls-Royce Vulture (the Tornado).

Mr Philip Lucas, who as a Hawker test pilot made the first flights on the Tornado, the Typhoon, the Tempest and the Fury, and now lives in retirement near Horsham, Sussex, recalled, 'The Vulture was so bad that it was scrapped in a decision taken at a meeting at Langley attended by, among others, Camm and senior officials of Rolls-Royce.

'It was underpowered, overweight, and mechanically at fault. The decision to scrap it led, paradoxically, to production of the magnificent Lancaster bomber — introduced to replace the Manchester, which had two Vultures. The decision was made also to concentrate on the Typhoon with the Sabre; but had it been known how little development had been done on this engine, and the problems which were to come, I wonder whether it would have been proceeded with?'

First flight of the Tornado took place on October 6, 1939, and of the Typhoon on February 24, 1940. Hawkers had received an instruction from the Air Ministry by late 1939 to proceed with the construction of 1,000 of their new fighters. The plan, drawn up in the summer of that year, was that the first should be delivered in July, 1940 — and the 500th by September, 1941! These forecasts were soon rewritten as problems with both types of engine became more and more apparent.

What finally killed the Tornado was the government demand to Rolls-Royce to work flat out on a new 12-cylinder engine, the Griffon, which, although much smaller and lighter than the 24-cylinder Vulture, developed about the same horsepower. Available stocks of Vultures were transferred to Manchester bomber production, but this twin-engined aircraft itself was rejected as under-powered after a near-disastrous period of operations, and was evolved into the Lancaster, powered by four Merlins.

Another blow to the Typhoon/Tornado programme was the decision by Lord Beaverbrook, as Minister of Aircraft Production, in May, 1940, to slow down development of all projects so that production could be concentrated on five types vital to the forthcoming Battle of Britain — the Hurricane and Spitfire, and the Wellington, Whitley and Blenheim bombers.

Nine months were virtually lost by Hawker until the 'stop' was taken off as, with the battle won, the production of Hurricanes from Hawker factories at Langley and Brooklands, and at Glosters, became slightly less vital. Within the 1,000 aircraft on order, 500 were to have been Tornados and 250 Typhoons, with the remainder left undecided until it was

seen which proved to have the best engine. The end of the Tornado came with only three prototypes actually constructed. These were used by Hawker and others for experimental testing.

One was later to become the first of the Hawker machines to be fitted with the Bristol Centaurus. Tornados were to have been constructed at the Manchester factory of A. V. Roe, Hawker having their hands full with Hurricane work. For this reason, only a few Typhoons were actually built at Langley, most of the production coming off the lines at the Gloster factory at Hucclecote, Gloucester.

So Typhoons, after several false starts, began to appear in the wartime skies over Britain — a new shape, hefty and menacing with its powerful body, enormous and characteristic chin radiator, and its considerable bulk — seven tons, as opposed to the four tons of the Hurricane, on which its lines clearly showed that it was based.

There was, too, a new sound — the bellow of its mighty Sabre engine. But for too many of its early pilots, there was the fear that this bellow would suddenly be replaced by silence. The Typhoon was almost ready to be pressed into service, but its problems were still a long way from being solved.

The 'one-ton' monster which powered the Typhoon, the Napier Sabre engine. The Sabre had tremendous technical problems right through its development, and into squadron service, and these were only completely eliminated towards the end of the war.

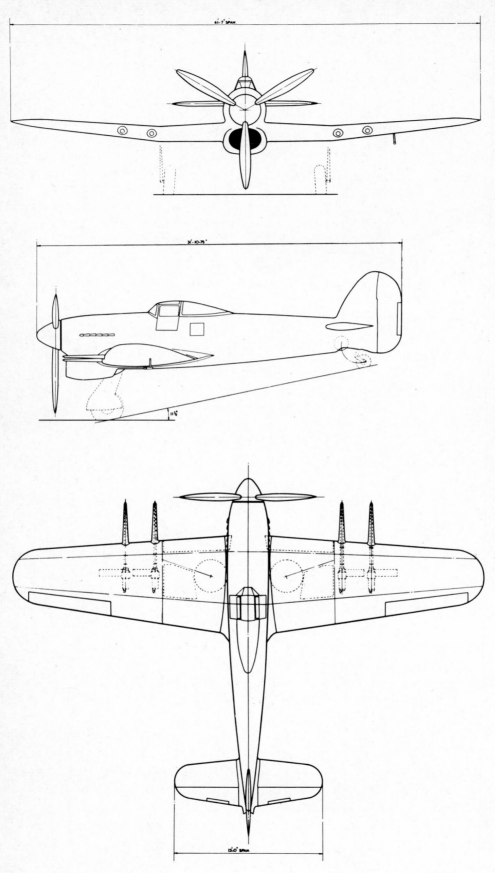

Left: A basic three-view drawing of the early Typhoon 1B produced by Hawkers during 1940-41. The company had insufficient design office staff to make detail drawings, and men were sent out to the prototype in between tests at the airfield at Langley to make sketches which could be turned into drawings from which production aircraft could be constructed.

Top right: Second Tornado prototype (first flight, December 5, 1940) has the 'big chin' look which was to become so familiar. It was powered by the R-R Vulture, but this engine was shortly afterwards cancelled because of the problems, particularly connecting bolt rod fractures, which had shown up on it in use on the Avro Manchester twin-engine bomber (which later, with four Merlins, became the Lancaster).

Middle and bottom right: A further Tornado prototype had a radial Bristol Centaurus engine fitted. It was first flown by Lucas on October 23, 1941. The aircraft was greatly modified during development, as can be seen from these two pictures in which the exhaust is exposed and then enclosed inside an unwieldy fairing, but Tornado development was eventually stopped. The lessons learned from experimenting with radial engines read across significantly to the later Tempest II and Sea Fury.

16

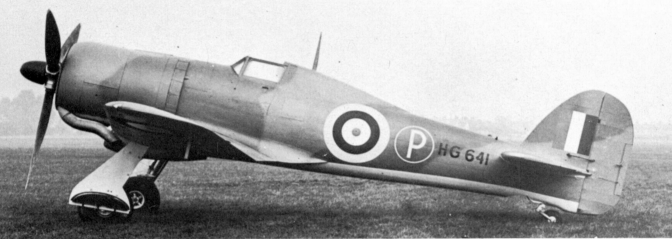

A Cat Out of the Bag

Under the conditions of strict wartime secrecy, only a handful of the British public knew about the Typhoon, and it was not until May 4, 1941, by which time the type had been flying for some 20 months, that the government propaganda machine let the cat out of the bag.

The *Sunday Chronicle* quoted Mr Lucas as commenting on the Typhoon, 'It's a winner from the word go.' But for those who were able to read between the lines, there was a hint of the troubles which he and his Hawker test pilot colleagues were encountering at that time. Mr Lucas was said to have added: 'If all machines were perfect the first time, I'd be out of a job.'

And another newspaper wrote, 'One of the biggest gambles British aircraft chiefs have ever taken was in putting it in production straight from the drawing board, before a practical flying test.'

Mr Lucas had gone to Hawker under the then chief test pilot George Bulman in 1931. As the development work on the Tornado/Typhoon accelerated, immense efforts to keep the programme a secret from the Germans were made by him and the whole staff at Langley. Despite this, the programme had its scares — such as one day when a set of engine installation drawings for the Sabre were stolen from the seat of the car belonging to a Napier engineer, parked inside the factory. That mystery was never solved.

Recalling the maiden flights, and the early test sorties which followed, Mr Lucas said, 'I had a pretty good idea of how the Typhoon airframe was going to perform, because I had already flown the Tornado. But the engine was an unknown quantity, and we were all deeply suspicious of it.

'One of the bad things about it was that it would not start. An engine with 24 cylinders took an awful lot of turning over, and it was discovered that there was a minimum speed to crank it before you got enough compression.

'On the day of the first flight, the wind was blowing in the wrong direction, and there was a certain amount of teeth-sucking until we decided to go — because of the urgency of the programme. Everything worked. The flight lasted for

30 minutes.' In Mr Lucas's log book the outing is laconically recorded, 'first flight' — although the entry is made in red ink.

Between February 24, and May 2, 1940, 74 flights were made, totalling 44 hours — an average of 36 minutes each. Mr Lucas recalls: 'The Typhoon was basically a magnificent aeroplane, very strong structurally. But the main problem was the engine. There was sleeve wear. Sleeves broke, pistons broke, and oil poured out of the engine, blinding the pilot.

'We had very few forced landings, but a lot of precautionary landings, because we were very experienced pilots, and we were on the watch all the time. The moment trouble started, we were back on the ground, and in the first 20 hours of flying, I had seven or eight of these precautionary landings. Another engine trouble was cooling. The oil in the engine had a circulation of 3,000 gallons an hour, and the temperature gauge used to go off the clock.'

It was during this early period of development flying, on May 9, 1940, that

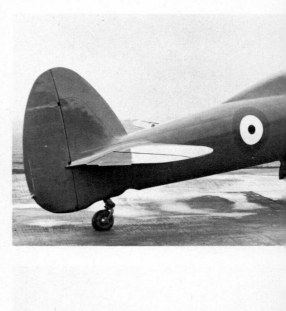

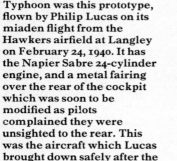

Top right: The very first Typhoon was this prototype, flown by Philip Lucas on its miaden flight from the Hawkers airfield at Langley on February 24, 1940. It has the Napier Sabre 24-cylinder engine, and a metal fairing over the rear of the cockpit which was soon to be modified as pilots complained they were unsighted to the rear. This was the aircraft which Lucas brought down safely after the fuselage split on a test flight.

Bottom right: The second prototype had hinged wheel flaps which folded after the undercarriage retracted to form a smooth underwing surface. In this picture the armament of 12 Browning machine guns can be clearly seen, and early production models were so armed due to a hold-up in the supply of cannon parts.

the Typhoon prototype being flown by Mr Lucas split its fuselage behind the cockpit. At the time he was diving the aircraft and yawing it from side to side, to detect directional instability. He remembered, 'You could see the sky through the side of the aircraft.'

Adhering to the test pilot's dictum that you must always try to get the aircraft back, so that what went wrong can be identified and put right, he nursed the stricken Typhoon down to a successful landing — after which, 'the whole aircraft sagged, and had to be taken away on a trolley.' It was a feat of courage and airmanship which was to earn him the George Medal.

Despite the extreme condition of the prototype, it was repaired. Less than a month later it was flying again. The incident had nothing to do with the later series of structural failings which dogged the Typhoon. The main problems during the early development stage continued to be thrown up by the engine, the official *History of the Second World War* describing the Sabre's record at that stage as one of the 'most melancholy stories' in the design and development of weapons in that conflict.

The main cause of the trouble was distortion of the clyinder sleeves. Even when Typhoons began going to the squadrons, the time between major overhauls of 25 hours as laid down was often not attained. Sleeves produced by Napier often failed to reach 20 hours when tested on the bench.

By 1943, with the problem still unsolved by Napier, and with production still lagging, the Ministry of Aircraft Production pushed through a marriage between that company and English Electric. At around the same time the Bristol engine company applied their expertise, it being discovered that their sleeves for the Taurus radial engine could be adapted by machining to Sabre size. While Napier sleeves were distorting after only 20 hours, Bristol sleeves lasted for 120 hours without any sign of real wear. A rapid decision was made to swing the production over, machine tools being obtained from the United States to give Napier the ability to bring their work up to standard.

Philip Lucas, who made the first flight in the Typhoon on February 24, 1940, safely landed the prototype on one of the test flights soon after despite this enormous split in the fuselage through which, he said, 'it was possible to see the sky'. Returning the new aircraft in one piece rather than baling out was vital to the future of the whole programme, and Lucas received the George Medal for his feat of courage and airmanship.

Above left: A rare shot of the early Typhoon with fared – in rear to the cockpit and 12 machine guns. The gull shape to the wings can be clearly seen. The photograph was taken by a Boscombe Down cameraman while the Typhoon was carrying out armament trials during September, 1941.

Left: The first Squadron Standard Typhoon of 609 squadron photographed in October, 1942. Note the improved rear vision.

Above: Large sections of the Typhoon wing opened up for the armourers to service the Hispano cannon, two on each side. The shells were stored in the metal ammunition boxes to the left of the guns, being carried on a belt feed into the circular feed mechanism, and from there into the breech. Rate of delivery from these formidable weapons was 760 shells a minute.

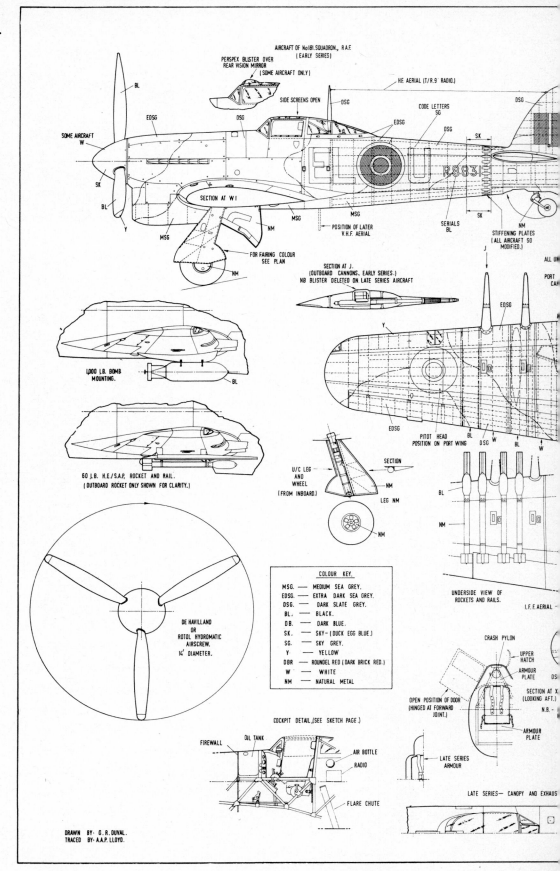

AIRCRAFT OF No.181.SQUADRON., R.A.F.
(EARLY SERIES)

PERSPEX BLISTER OVER
REAR VISION MIRROR
(SOME AIRCRAFT ONLY)

H.F. AERIAL (T/R.9 RADIO.)

SIDE SCREENS OPEN

CODE LETTERS
SG

SOME AIRCRAFT
W

POSITION OF LATER
V.H.F. AERIAL

SERIALS
BL

STIFFENING PLATES
(ALL AIRCRAFT SO
MODIFIED.)

FOR FAIRING COLOUR
SEE PLAN

SECTION AT J.
(OUTBOARD CANNONS. EARLY SERIES.)
NB BLISTER DELETED ON LATE SERIES AIRCRAFT

1,000 L.B. BOMB
MOUNTING.

60 L.B. H.E./S.A.P. ROCKET AND RAIL.
(OUTBOARD ROCKET ONLY SHOWN FOR CLARITY.)

PITOT HEAD
POSITION ON PORT WING

U/C LEG
AND
WHEEL
(FROM INBOARD.)

SECTION

LEG NM

UNDERSIDE VIEW OF
ROCKETS AND RAILS.

I.F.F. AERIAL

DE HAVILLAND
OR
ROTOL HYDROMATIC
AIRSCREW.
14' DIAMETER.

COLOUR KEY.

MSG. — MEDIUM SEA GREY.
EDSG. — EXTRA DARK SEA GREY.
DSG. — DARK SLATE GREY.
BL. — BLACK.
DB. — DARK BLUE.
SK. — SKY- (DUCK EGG BLUE.)
SG. — SKY GREY.
Y. — YELLOW
DBR — ROUNDEL RED (DARK BRICK RED.)
W — WHITE
NM — NATURAL METAL

CRASH PYLON

UPPER
HATCH

ARMOUR
PLATE

OPEN POSITION OF DOOR
(HINGED AT FORWARD
JOINT.)

SECTION AT X
(LOOKING AFT.)

LATE SERIES
ARMOUR

ARMOUR
PLATE

COCKPIT DETAIL (SEE SKETCH PAGE.)

FIREWALL

OIL TANK

AIR BOTTLE

RADIO

FLARE CHUTE

LATE SERIES— CANOPY AND EXHAUS

DRAWN BY. G. R. DUVAL.
TRACED BY. A.A.P. LLOYD.

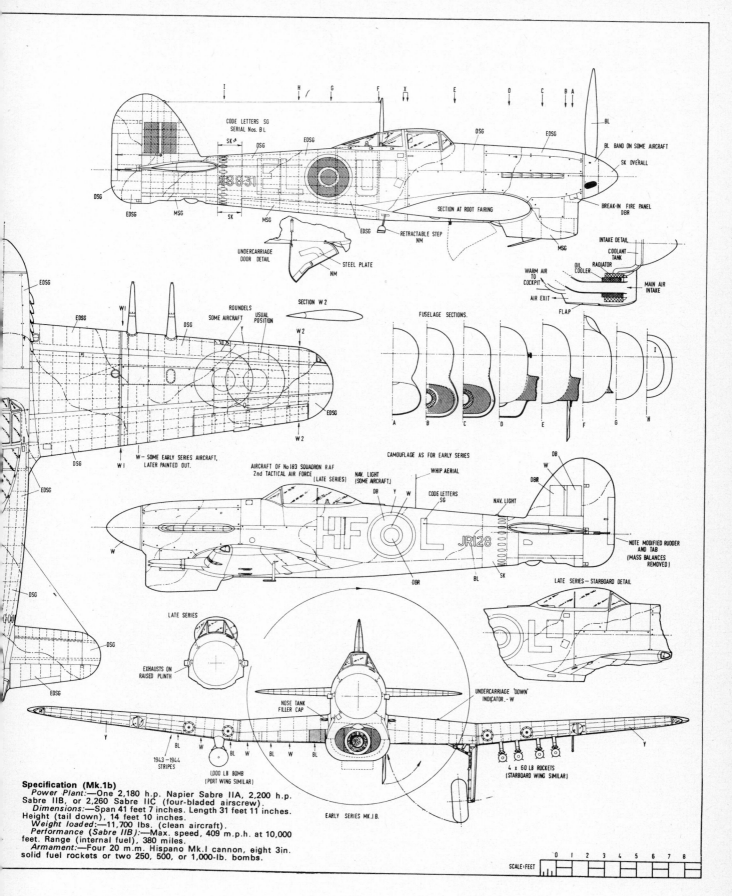

CODE LETTERS SG
SERIAL Nos. B L

BL

BL BAND ON SOME AIRCRAFT

SK OVERALL

BREAK-IN FIRE PANEL
DBR

INTAKE DETAIL

COOLANT TANK
OIL COOLER
RADIATOR
WARM AIR TO COCKPIT
MAIN AIR INTAKE
AIR EXIT
FLAP

SECTION AT ROOT FAIRING

RETRACTABLE STEP
NM

UNDERCARRIAGE DOOR DETAIL

STEEL PLATE
NM

SECTION W 2

ROUNDELS
SOME AIRCRAFT
USUAL POSITION

FUSELAGE SECTIONS.

W— SOME EARLY SERIES AIRCRAFT, LATER PAINTED OUT.

CAMOUFLAGE AS FOR EARLY SERIES

AIRCRAFT OF No 183 SQUADRON R A F
2nd TACTICAL AIR FORCE
(LATE SERIES)

NAV. LIGHT
(SOME AIRCRAFT.)

WHIP AERIAL

CODE LETTERS SG

NAV. LIGHT

JR128

NOTE MODIFIED RUDDER AND TAB
(MASS BALANCES REMOVED)

LATE SERIES — STARBOARD DETAIL

LATE SERIES

EXHAUSTS ON RAISED PLINTH

NOSE TANK FILLER CAP

UNDERCARRIAGE 'DOWN' INDICATOR.- W

EARLY SERIES MK.I B.

1943-1944 STRIPES

1,000 LB BOMB
(PORT WING SIMILAR)

4 x 60 LB ROCKETS
(STARBOARD WING SIMILAR)

Specification (Mk.1b)

Power Plant:—One 2,180 h.p. Napier Sabre IIA, 2,200 h.p. Sabre IIB, or 2,260 Sabre IIC (four-bladed airscrew).

Dimensions:—Span 41 feet 7 inches. Length 31 feet 11 inches. Height (tail down), 14 feet 10 inches.

Weight loaded:—11,700 lbs. (clean aircraft).

Performance (Sabre IIB):—Max. speed, 409 m.p.h. at 10,000 feet. Range (internal fuel), 380 miles.

Armament:—Four 20 m.m. Hispano Mk.I cannon, eight 3in. solid fuel rockets or two 250, 500, or 1,000-lb. bombs.

SCALE-FEET   0 1 2 3 4 5 6 7 8

Sorting out the
Problems

John W. R. Taylor, today an internationally-known aviation journalist, was intimately associated with the technical troubles of the Typhoon as a young draughtsman at Hawkers in 1941-42. He recalled: 'When I first went there as a trainee in March 1941, one of the first things that Camm did was to take me over to the experimental shop where the Tornado and Typhoon prototypes were parked side by side. To see those enormous fighters sitting there, with their wide-track undercarriages and great open-mouth radiators, was tremendously impressive.

'By the end of that year the Typhoon was having a lot of trouble. Almost every airfield in East Anglia seemed to have its own 'Tiffie glider' — a Typhoon which had suffered failure of its Sabre engine and had force-landed. The airframe was plagued with snags as well — in addition to the tail troubles — so Hawkers formed a Defects Department under Ted Major, now general manager support services with BOAC, with Maurice Allward and myself as his assistants.

'The sort of problems which we were asked to sort out had caused a member of a Typhoon squadron returning from a sortie over France to dive, apparently without cause, into the Channel. We reasoned that the pilot, who was very experienced, must have turned the fuel cock in the cockpit the wrong way when dropping his long-range tanks, so jettisoning all his wing fuel as well. Yet this seemed impossible to understand, as markings on the cock indicated clearly when it had been turned to the right position for dropping the tanks.

'I sat in the cockpit of a Typhoon and went through the tank-dropping procedure time after time. Eventually I tried it all again, on the assumption that the pilot might be looking behind him for enemy fighters while turning the fuel cock. Glancing across at the markings on the control while my head was craned to the other side of the canopy, it became clear that the effect of parallax might cause the pilot to turn the control the wrong way. We repositioned the cock about five degrees, and there was no more trouble of this kind.

'Camm's proud boast was of the small numbers who achieved so much in the Hawker drawing office right through the war years; but this meant that often no senior people could be spared for a new project. This was the case when it was decided to develop a night-fighter version of the Typhoon, and the job of producing virtually all the design drawings was given to me. It was decided to take out the fuel tank from the port wing,

The men who had the task of test-flying the Typhoon and helping to iron out its snags are pictured here, in March, 1941, outside Old Timbers, the cottage just at the edge of the Hawkers airfield at Langley used as a pilots' mess. From left to right they are, George Bulman (chief test pilot), Bill Humble, Hubert Broad (chief production test pilot), Frank Fox, Philip Lucas (deputy chief test pilot), Merryck Hymans, Mr Pegg, Frank Silk, and Roland Beamont.

replacing the lost capacity with tanks under the wings, and to fill the tank bay with three radar sets. The aerials were half-buried in the wingtips, and there were other modifications to suit the aircraft for a night role, such as fitting flame-damping exhausts. Camm was keenly interested in the project, which represented our first attempt to give the pilot a radar on which he could pick up enemy intruders independently of ground stations. A prototype was built and flown, but then the whole plan was dropped.

'Meanwhile, Hawkers had been developing the Tempest, which went against former Air Ministry policy that all fuel had to be carried in the wings. This was not possible in the thin wings of the Tempest; so Hawkers fitted a large fuselage tank in front of the cockpit. It had been intended to call the new aircraft the Typhoon II, but installing the fuselage tank meant that it had a longer nose; this in turn meant that it needed a dorsal fin to increase the tail area. By this time it had become so different from the Typhoon that it was given a new name.

'With the Tempest there was again a problem of shortage of drawing office staff. There were never enough people to handle all the detail drawings; so the basic airframe was designed in the usual way but some of the 'plumbing' and equipment were installed by the experimental workshop staff in what seemed to be the best places, without the work being covered by drawings. The result was that we had one very nice prototype Tempest at Langley, but could not build any more like it because there were no drawings of many of the installations. So I was sent down to Langley under the remote control of Assistant Chief Draughtsman Tommy Wake, to 'productionise' the aircraft — that is to make drawings on the spot which could be sent back to Kingston and converted into production drawings in the less frantic atmosphere of the design office.

'It involved clambering over the prototype between flights, so that everything not covered by drawings could be measured up extremely accurately and drawn in intelligible form. The pressure was enormous, and I remember finding one day a senior member of the project office, who later became one of Britain's leading fighter designers himself, climbing over the aircraft with a handful of plasticine, remodelling some of the fairings. With the design undergoing constant refinement in this way, it was an exciting and challenging experience for a twenty-year-old.

'Without any doubt, Camm taught me all I know about aircraft engineering. He was a perfectionist and a demanding man. I once heard him compared, aptly, with the great conductor of an orchestra, who could not necessarily play the individual instruments as well as those he had trained, but who could produce the finest music in the world from his blend of players. He held the chief designer's post at Hawkers for more than 40 years, and during all that time the only aircraft which suffered structural failure was the Typhoon. This could have happened to any aeroplane at a time when so little was known about metal fatigue, especially one with a great thick wing, which was pushing against the 'sonic barrier' for the first time — and the Americans were encountering similar problems with their P-38 Lightning.'

Right and below: One Typhoon prototype was developed by Hawkers as a night interceptor, with one of the wing fuel tanks removed and replaced by an underwing tank, and the space used for radar which was to guide the pilot on to intruding Germans. Aerials were partially buried in the wings, and the engine exhaust was damped so that it did not give away tell-tale flames at night. The version was not proceeded with, mainly because it was considered that flying a Typhoon at night while operating radar would have put too much workload on the pilot.

Close-up showing the in-wing camera installation of a photo-reconnaissance Typhoon. The feed of one of the aircraft's cannons is situated in the adjoining compartment.

The Line of Vision

In addition to the doleful saga of the engine, and the structural failure troubles in the tail which were to follow, the early Typhoon flying showed up other basic design snags. Some of these were cured relatively easily, some took a long time to identify and beat, while a few remained with the Typhoon for the whole of its life in service.

The most serious of these, in view of the fact that the aircraft had been designed originally as a high-altitude fighter, able to climb at a high rate of knots, intercept enemy bomber and fighter formations, and then outfly them at great heights, was its lack of performance above 20,000 feet. This factor went close to bringing the whole project to cancellation, although — ironically — it was the aircraft's remarkably good performance at heights

below this level which saved it, and made it a legend in the history of air warfare.

Hawker had estimated early in the development phase that their new aircraft would have a maximum level speed in excess of 460mph. The Air Ministry reduced this forecast to 428mph, but in the event, early Typhoons were only just able to top 400mph. Later versions of the Sabre engine boosted this straight and level performance to 412mph.

Pilots who flew the Typhoon early in its life were highly critical of the view which they were afforded from the cockpit. It appalled them to find that they were quite unable to keep a lookout to the rear, the portion of the fairing behind their heads being covered in with metal. Thick windscreen pillars marred the view to the front, while access to the cockpit was through a door which appeared to bear more affinity to the current range of Austin Seven cars than a marque of fighters.

Enormous pressure was placed on Hawker and the Ministry of Aircraft Production to improve the rearwards field of view, and in spite of reluctance to introduce any modifications which would slow production at such a crucial time, the metal-covered portion at the back of the pilot's head was glazed. Later production standard Typhoon 1Bs had a newly-designed one-piece bubble hood which could be slid back on rails, giving the pilots almost perfect vision over 360 degrees.

Why did the early Typhoons appear with such a restricted view? The opinion remains that it was more than just a design quirk; rather a whole battle philosophy which inadvertently produced a cockpit from which the first intimation a pilot would have had that an enemy was on his tail was when he was being hit. At the time that the Tornado and Typhoon were going on to the drawing board the feeling in the places where high strategy was decided was that, with the speeds of 400mph which this new generation would have, dogfights of the classic kind seen in the first world war, and which were still an essential part of RAF training in biplanes, would be extinct.

Combining with their high intercept speeds a hitherto unbelievably heavy firepower, the Tornado/Typhoon series would, it was believed, attack in impeccable squadron formation, overshooting by miles before turning in a wide arc to mount a second pass — if it remained necessary. Meanwhile, the enemy fighters would be left behind, completely outpaced. How fallacious this thinking was can be seen today, 40 years later, when air forces all over the world are buying simple, unsophisticated fighters with one overriding attribute — an ability to hold their own in dogfights.

A second worrying problem for those who flew the early Typhoons was, yet again, connected with the Sabre engine — vibration. This had nothing to do with the frequent failures, making itself felt when the engine was running sweetly. It was not apparent on the ground, but manifested itself as soon as the Typhoon took off as a high-frequency shake which was so pronounced that many pilots feared it would affect their virility. Vibrometers were attached to the prototypes to measure the shock, and the worst of the trouble was later smoothed out through the installation of a specially-sprung seat for the pilot, and by more accurately balancing the propellers.

A further worry was the way in which carbon monoxide from the 24 cylinders of the Sabre engine would seep into the cockpit through the firewall bulkhead between it and the engine compartment. This led to an instruction to pilots to put on their oxygen masks as soon as they started up the engine on the ground,

a procedure which would not normally be followed until they reached 12,000 feet or so.

The mechanism which fed the shells into the cannons also gave rise to frequent anxiety. A Belgian pilot serving with one of the first RAF squadrons to receive Typhoons in service had his guns go off while he was still on the ground, and without pressing the trigger. Fortunately, the only damage was to the fabric of a maintenance hangar at RAF Duxford.

Most of these basic flaws in the aircraft were still with it when it went to the RAF with first deliveries taking place during July, 1941. The first squadrons to receive Typhoons were 56 and 609, at Duxford, in September of that year. Only in time of war would any new aircraft have been pressed into operations while still so unprepared, but as Mr Philip Lucas, the Typhoon's first test pilot, later commented, 'In those days, you could not wait for perfection. You had to make up your mind just how far you could go, and then back your judgement.'

Left: By January, 1943, Typhoons were with the squadrons, and had the more reliable Sabre II engine. The rear vision had been progressively improved, first with extra transparent panels and then, as in this picture, a clear-view rear panel.

Below: In a further modification, seen in close-up the cockpit cover was converted into a 'bubble' which slid backwards for access, so transforming what had been limited vision into a magnificent all-round view. By the end of 1943, most Typhoons had this important modification, as did all the Tempests.

Flying the Typhoon

Beamont described his first Typhoon flight as follows:

At first sight the Typhoon was a heavy-looking, rather cumbersome aeroplane and, so maintained many Spitfire pilots, it was at second sight! Nevertheless, at closer acquaintance it was seen to be an immensely rugged aeroplane with a thick, high-lift wing of generous area, and an impressive Napier Sabre engine of almost twice the power of the Merlin in the Hurricane, which it had been designed to replace.

With four 20mm Hispano cannon protruding far out from the wing leading-edge and a top speed said to be in excess of 400mph — that is around 100mph faster than a Hurricane — it was certainly intriguing and I lost no time in persuading Philip Lucas, Hawker's acting Chief Test Pilot at the time, of my urgent need to fly one.

This was arranged at Langley on March 8, 1942, and it turned out to be a memorable occasion.

The Typhoon I was to fly was an early pre-production aircraft, serial no R7681, and one mounted it via a telescopic, retracting footrest behind the starboard wing trailing-edge; on to the wing root and from thence into the cockpit through a car-type door complete with wind-down window. With this and its associated side-hinged roof panel closed, the pilot had an immediate impression of being behind bars, the proportion of metal work to transparency being so predominent in all significant directions as to make one wonder if it could be useful as a fighter at all.

But one sat high in this big aeroplane, and the long wings with cannons sprouting forward, the enormous nose and vast three-blade propeller, gave an immediate impression of power and strength.

In common with the conventions of the period, most of the basic pilot operations were simple, with manual, cable-operated controls, on-off fuel system, and hydraulics limited to undercarriage and flap; but the engine needed some attention.

The 24-cylinder Sabre was felt to be too large for practical electric starting in a fighter, and so it had been provided with a Coffman cartridge starter which went off with an impressive explosion but did not always start the engine.

This was because the Sabre proved temperamental and extremely sensitive to temperature variations when starting, to the extent that although the pilots' notes gave detailed directions on throttle setting and number of primes with the Kigas pump, these proved inadequate to cover the wide range of temperatures experienced with cold and hot engines, in summer and winter.

Ground crews and pilots tended to learn the peculiarities of their own aircraft in this respect, but there could be no standard drill because it soon became apparent that there were also subtle variations between the characteristics of one aircraft and the next.

Generally, for a cold start the throttle was set at about 1½in open, with propeller pitch at FINE, and after building up pressure, the person in the cockpit gave two full primes on the Kigas. Then, with the oil-dilution switch pressed (to inject petrol into the cold congealing engine oil) the Coffman switch was operated. If the engine fired, it was coaxed into life by 'keeping it going on the primer' until with gentle adjustment it could be held on the throttle. All this activity was accompanied by sheets of exhaust smoke which continued until the Sabre was warm enough to run smoothly at 2,100rpm

If it failed to start, another half-stroke of the Kigas was tried and the second Coffman cartridge fired. There was a third cartridge for a final attempt, but when used it often blew a 'safety disc'. When that happened, the disc had to be replaced, the starter cooled and reloaded, the engine 'blown-out' by hand-turning the propeller with fuel cock off to expel surplus fuel from the manifold and plugs — after which the procedure was started again.

Eventually, pilots learnt how to cover most conditions, but severe cold or hot re-starts generally produced problems and there were often one or more Typhoons left banging away at dispersal when a squadron taxied out for take-off.

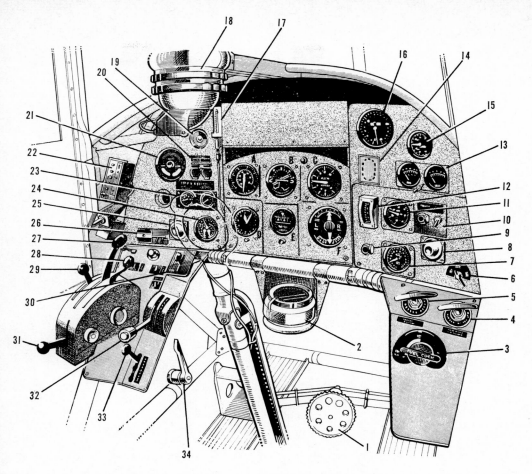

However, on this first occasion for me, experimental test pilot Bill Humble set up the starting procedure and the Sabre burst into life first time, to the accompaniment of clouds of acrid smoke.

Humble had briefed me that the aircraft was straightforward to fly and land, in accordance with the figures in the pilots' notes, but that propeller torque gave it a powerful swing on take-off and that I should set full rudder trim against this. So, having set it up and also moved the elevator trimmer to neutral, I opened up gently to start taxying away from the tarmac on to the rough grass of Langley aerodrome.

The wide-track undercarriage and soft-operating brakes resulted in easy control on the ground, and vision of the boundary was still available over the nose so that one could taxy in the direction one wanted, which was a change from Spitfires.

At the southern boundary for a take-off into a light north easterly wind I

ran up the Sabre against the brakes until they began to slip and the noise, vibration and general commotion were becoming impressive. Then, with temperature and pressures correct, I released the brakes to begin a take-off which has remained memorable over a quarter of a century.

The engine noise was tremendous as the tail lifted normally to forward stick, but almost immediately the Typhoon began to veer to starboard. Feeding on port rudder straightened things for a moment, but it then became obvious that the situation was somewhat critical. Despite full port rudder and maximum left leg effort, the Typhoon was already veering off 30 degrees to starboard from the narrow grass strip — straight towards the factory buildings of the Holme Wood works — and it was still on the ground.

An instant decision of some sort being urgently necessary, I judged that trying to stop before hitting the factory would not be profitable. So I hauled back on the stick and at the same time went for the

Among the experiments carried out on the Typhoon was the fitting of its in-line Sabre engine with a radial cowling. The object here was to incorporate the radiator within the cowl, so doing away with the bulky chin radiator, and so reducing drag and making the aircraft go faster. One Typhoon IB was used by Napiers for these experiments, but they were not taken into production.

rudder trim, which I knew I had set to full bias. Two things then happened. Firstly the Typhoon clambered into the air and roared a few feet over the factory buildings, at least 40 degrees off the runway heading; secondly, there was instant response to winding the trimmer in the opposite direction! Somehow I had set it in the opposite sense to the correct one.

With flaps and undercarriage retracted, and rpm and throttle set to climb power at 3,450rpm, speed increased rapidly in a shallow climb until we had 300mph indicated passing 2,000 feet.

Stability and control were excellent, with good damping, and in combat manoeuvres I felt that the Typhoon showed good promise for so large a fighter. Particularly impressive was gun-aiming stability, and even in a ground attack type dive into rough air at low level with 400mph on the ASI, the gunsight aiming spot could be held well on the target.

In a clattering but impressive full-power zoom climb, we went back to about 15,000ft for a dive to the pilots' notes limit of 500mph.

This came up quickly in a 30 degree dive and was impressive for high vibration and noise level in the cockpit. Damping on all axes remained good but, although control forces were heavying up, there was still adequate con-

The good stability and damping on all axes, coupled with pleasantly responsive controls down to touch-down, and the wide-tracked security of the under-carriage, with view unimpaired over the nose when the tailwheel was on the ground, all added up to an easier operation by far than landing a Spitfire. I felt at once that this aeroplane had potential for bad weather and night operation, in addition to being sub-stantially faster than most other fighters at low level.

At much above 20,000 feet its performance and manoevrability were less than those of the current Spitfires, 109s and new Fw 190. Below this level I felt that the Typoon could well have the advantage — but something would have to be done about those car-type windows!

RPB

Chris Wren, the well-known aviation cartoonist, gave the new Typhoon pugnacious human qualities in this delightful drawing and verse for The Aeroplane magazine. Compared with the Camel and the Hurricane, the Typhoon, Wren rhymed, was, 'Faster, more deadly, and full of fight.'

Sopwith, Hawker, what names of great tradition !
The Camel and Hurricane, these we know,
Rarely is there found such an exposition
Of glorious service 'gainst common foe —
And now, before proud British eye,
Faster, more deadly, and full of fight,
The Typhoon rages through the sky,
Epitomising the Allied might.

trollability in pitch and roll for combat to be practical at this speed, especially as gun-aiming stability seemed un-impaired.

Aerobatics in the rolling plane proved pleasant and precise, as they did in the looping plane although it seemed that about 3,000 feet would be needed for a full loop, at least until one got to know the aircraft better.

Then back into the circuit, where the Typhoon could be set up easily in the then popular continuous-curve 'Spitfire' approach at 120mph with wheels and flaps down, rolling out on to 'short finals' at 95mph for an easy hold-off with elevator in hand, and a three-point landing at about 75mph.

The View from the Ground

Sydney Hanson, a retired RAF flight lieutenant, was a sergeant fitter with B Flight of 609 Squadron in 1943, and was in the forefront of the battle to eradicate the dreadful snags which were making the Sabre engine so unreliable, and were placing a question mark over the whole future of the Typhoon as an aircraft type. He recalled, 'We had got so used to Merlins that we could do anything with them. Then we were sent this one-ton monster, and it suddenly became very hard going.

'For a start, it had 48 spark plugs; but its main troubles were that it used to melt its pistons, its sleeves would seize up into the engine block. It was also very difficult to start — especially in the mornings, after a cold night. In theory, the engine as it was designed shouldn't have started at all. When it did, it made a noise which I shall always remember as the sound of tearing calico.

'The trouble with starting was that the Coffmann starter which had been designed for Spitfires and Hurricanes was not really powerful enough to start the Typhoon. We overcame the problem of premature reigning-up by changing the priming mixture from the traditional 100 percent petrol to 70 percent petrol and 30 percent oil, so stopping the oil from being washed out of the cylinders. And in winter we would have a ground crew on duty all night, whose job was to start and warm up all the engines in the squadron four times between dusk and dawn.

'This was at Lympne, and the noise of these night-time activities so disturbed the local residents that they wrote to the commanding officer of 609, Squadron Leader Pat Thornton-Browne, complaining about it. He wrote back to them, offering the choice of being disturbed by Typhoons or Fw 190s and after that we heard no more complaints. From the point of view of the ground crews, the Typhoon was a specialist aircraft which you had to grow up with, while getting used to its special snags. The engine was high-revving, and we had to get the snags out while it was in operational service.

'There was an added urgency in what

we were doing, because the Typhoon's main role at the time was patrolling against the 190s at a height of only 200 feet between Dungeness and North Foreland. The Typhoon used to overtake the 190s like an express train at that height, and its four cannons used to blast them out of the sky. But when an engine cut at that height there was not much chance of getting out.

'It certainly was a tough aircraft, and used to take a hell of a lot of punishment — the sort of punishment which would have finished off other fighters. One of

our pilots pursued a 190 over France at very low level and came back with half a forest in his radiator. Another, returning from a sweep over Europe, was seen by the rest of the formation to break away and go into the sea. Back at the mess, the other pilots were having a drink when the police rang to ask that arrangements should be made to collect our man. 'His body'?, the police were asked. 'No. He's OK.', they replied. It seemed that the Typhoon had been so tough that it had not broken up on hitting the sea, but had sunk in one piece to the bottom, 50 feet

down. The pilot had then released himself and floated to the surface in an air bubble, little the worse for his exprience.

'One of the Typhoon's other little tricks, before we got wise to it, was to fire off its rockets automatically on the ground when the engine was started, due to a confusion of the electrical circuits. Luckily, no damage was ever done in this way, and we used to prevent it from happening by connecting up the rocket firing circuit only after the engine was running well.'

The monster exposed. Part of the engine cowling of a Typhoon is removed to reveal the top half of the massive – and troublesome – Napier Sabre engine. On the fuselage just to the rear a squadron artist has depicted a Nazi swastika being shattered by a diving Typhoon.

45

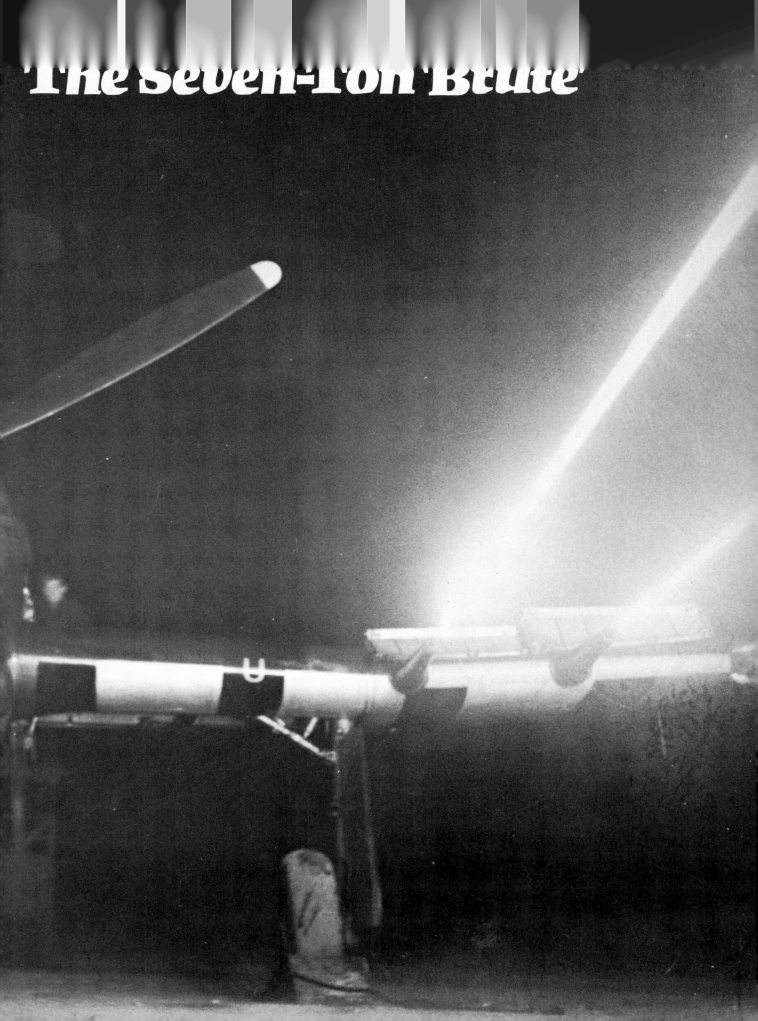

The Seven-Ton Brute

The reputation of the Typhoon had preceded it to the squadrons. It was hardly surprising that the majority of those pilots who were detailed to re-equip with it would have preferred to remain with their Spitfires and their Hurricanes. For while in theory it was an exciting event for any fighter pilot to be given the Service's latest fighter — the first to pierce the magic 400mph barrier — enthusiasm was dampened by the 'word' that had spread through the RAF bush telegraph that the Typhoon was a 'brute' — difficult to handle on take-off and landing, unforgiving in flight, and racked with technical problems which were resulting frequently in forced landings, or mid-air disintegration with no chance to use a parachute.

Hurricanes and Spitfires were 'gentlemen's aeroplanes', sweet and docile in operation, proven technically over six years of development and battle, and most unlikely to cut their engines just when you needed them the most, or to snap off their tails during some innocuous manoeuvre. In addition, the Hurricane and Spitfire 'looked right' — especially the Spitfire — streamlined and elegant, and at four tons just the right size to flip about the sky in dogfights with the enemy. So it was that the men of 56 and 609 Squadrons approached their new seven-ton charges — with their squat, bulky and powerful appearance heightened by the gigantic spinner and enormous chin radiator — with a mixture of interest and trepidation.

Many were heard to express the view in those early days of squadron service that, although they continued to be prepared to risk their lives against the enemy, they were not prepared to have themselves killed flying lousy equipment — and that was what most of them thought they had. After only a few days of trial, the opinion was general that their new equipment was not really fit to go to war in.

Although the Typhoon was now with the squadrons, it remained non-operational because of the repeated snags, and because maintenance had to be carried out so frequently. The early squadrons considered themselves fortunate if they could muster three serviceable aircraft at any one time. The pilots flew it, but they were almost universal in their criticisms of its heavy controls, the poor vision from the cockpit, and its inferior performance above 20,000 feet compared with that of the Spitfire.

Training in formation began gingerly, with the pilots on tenterhooks for the first sign of trouble from ether end of their new mounts. Often these formations would split up after only a few moments in the air as engines showed signs of spluttering, or oil started to rain on the windscreen, and forced landings in the nearest open space were carried out precipitately.

One other problem which showed itself at this time was the occasional inability of pilots from other RAF squadrons still flying Spitfires and Hurricanes to distinguish the Typhoon from the Luftwaffe's latest fighter, the Focke Wulf 190. Even though the 190 had a radial engine, the British fliers were sometimes fooled into thinking that the Typhoon was a German aircraft in the split-seconds before going into action, due to the heavy appearance given to its front end by the big radiator, and by the similarity of the wings. As a result, at least two Typhoons were lost during the early days of squadron service through attacks by Spitfires, while Thornton-Browne, CO of 609 Squadron, was shot down and killed by American Thunderbolts.

To aid instant recognition, the Typhoons were given white painted noses and engine cowlings for a time, making them look even more elephantine and ugly.

Ironically, it was the Fw 190 which proved to be the saviour of the Typhoon enabling it to prove that its true role was not going to be at high altitude, as had been planned from the drawing board, but as a low-level interceptor and ground attacker. With the Battle of Britain over and won by the end of 1940, and a lull in the air fighting setting in, the RAF began to send their fighters up on vast sweeps over France. These operations had a threefold aim — to give the Service continuing experience, to keep the

Germans busy, and to try to put some heart into the captive peoples on the ground below.

The new Typhoon squadrons were sent to join these sweeps; but it was soon embarrassingly proved that at the high altitudes at which the missions were being conducted they lacked essential engine power to outfly the representatives of a previous generation of fighters — the Spitfires.

This situation produced a split in policy thinking within the RAF, with a strong anti-Typhoon faction emerging to recommend that the whole project should be scrapped. At that time, however, the 190s were beginning to come over Britain in increasing numbers, and with increasing audacity, operating in bad weather and at low level on sneak hit-and-run raids, often on south coast targets. The older fighters could do little to stop such attacks.

Typhoons, with their greater speed at low level and their ability to turn inside the 190s, began intercepting these raids with success and knocking the intruders down. They, too, were able to fly in the worst weather, using bases strung out along the coast in the south-east corner of Britain, such as Manston, Ford, Tangmere and Thorney Island, and also in the west country.

The battle between the two Typhoon camps — with the 'antis' wanting it scrapped because of its lack of performance at high altitude, and the 'pros' urgings its continuation because they could see that it would come into its own in the offensive, rather than defensive, operations of the war years ahead — came to a climax at a meeting at Fighter Command, Bentley Priory.

Roland Beamont, then a squadron leader and CO of 609 Squadron, was at that meeting, and recalls that the main opposition came from the engineering branch, who were having a terrible time keeping the Typhoon flying. Their onslaught was led by the late Gordon Findlay, a Spitfire pilot and a specialist engineering officer at 11 Group.

'Findlay made an impassioned speech, shooting the Typhoon down on engineering grounds. When it was my turn to speak, I questioned whether Findlay had ever flown the Typhoon, which produced a stir round the table. I said that I had, and described how it behaved in operational service, and how it could be expected to perform in the future. The Commander-in Chief, Leigh-Mallory, made some remarks at the end of the meeting which appeared to be kind to me and the Typhhon, and we heard no more about the cancellation of the aircraft after that.

'A decision was obviously made to keep it in service as the ground attack aircraft of the future. At the meeting, I had said what was in my mind with considerable force, and emphasised that I was amazed that anybody should want to kill this aeroplane, which I thought was going to be extremely good.

Below: As if to prove the ruggedness of the original Camm design, RAF ground crew members pack the wings and fuselage of a Typhoon for an Air Ministry propaganda exercise. A rough count shows there are around 60 aboard – including a solitary WAAF!

Bottom: A remarkable shot taken at night – presumably with a remotely-controlled camera – of a Typhoon's four cannon being test-fired on the ground. The wartime caption gives the rate of fire as 80 shells in two seconds.

Above: The sort of view which German bomber-gunners had of a Typhoon as it attacked. This was, in fact, a peaceful excercise, and the picture was taken from the rear upper turret of a Handley Page Hampden.

Right: Painting of black and white stripes on the undersides of Typhoons did not solve the problem of mistaken identity between these aircraft and Fw190s by Allied ground forces. In an attempt to make Typhoons even more recognizable, some were painted white over their noses and radiators.

'I had enough confidence to say that, in spite of the fact that it had a bad technical reputation, I thought it would be a 'goer'. I knew of no other aircraft in service or envisaged which could provide the ground attack capability that we were going to need for the rest of the war, other than through a massive purchase from America.

'The Spitfire was a tremendous medium and high-altitude combat fighter, but it could not carry very much armament, and it was not very strong for ground attack. Also, it had poor visibility. The Hurricane was better, but by that time it was getting a bit outmoded for speed. I am sure that the Americans would have built us enough aeroplanes to do the job, but they would probably not have done it so well, and our successes in the Falaise gap and similar operations would not have been won so effectively. The enemy's losses would not have been so great, the attrition would have lasted much longer, and the period from D-Day to the end of the war would have been drawn out.'

Tail Problems

Tails kept snapping off Typhoons because — it was eventually discovered — when the aircraft encountered a severe gust and certain other flying conditions coincided, flutter was induced in the elevators which rapidly became so strong that it ripped apart even the immensely tough structure designed by Camm. The trouble was isolated to the mass balance of the elevator, which was suspended on a rod protruding forward beneath the tail-plane and which suffered metal fatigue. The balance was moved to a more conventional place within the elevator, and the problem was solved literally overnight.

Until the fault was traced and the modification introduced, Hawker and the RAF found themselves with one of the most puzzling and frightening mysteries in the history of aviation development. Before the 'fix', no fewer than 28 Typhoons dived to earth having suffered a massive failure of the rear of the fuselage. At most, only two of the pilots survived.

There was obviously little or no chance of getting out alive, for the failures occurred with no set pattern, at differing heights, and certainly not during the high-powered manoeuvres which could have been expected to put a strain on the fuselage. Some happened during a gentle cruise; others as an aircraft was approaching an airfield ready to land. Roland Beamont recalls one that occurred before his eyes: 'We were in a wing formation, about 24 Typhoons, when all of a sudden, one of the chaps in front of me stopped being a Typhoon and became a mass of little bits flying past. There was no doubt (Beamont added) that, as a result of these incidents, some of the pilots who were not the strongest brethren were becoming troubled'.

Such incidents happened without a second's warning. The pilots had neither time to bail out, nor to radio any message to the ground indicating what was happening — even if they could have known. So, while the Typhoon remained in squadron service, the whole baffling problem was thrown back to the test pilots at the Hawker airfield at Langley. They had the daunting task of taking up their aircraft day after day and, coldly and calculatingly, trying to make a tail break away, in the full knowledge that if they succeeded they would almost certainly not live to tell about it. Their mission would have been accomplished, however, as each flight was carried out to a planned schedule and those remaining on the ground knew exactly what type of flying was to be accomplished on that particular sortie.

Had one of these test Typhoons crashed with a tail failure, the pilot would very probably have died, but the men who stayed behind would have been able to identify with fair exactitude at what phase of flight the breakage had occurred. Armed with this knowledge, they would then have hoped to isolate the cause. Almost unbelievably, the Typhoon test aircraft were not fitted with air-to-ground radio. If a forced landing was made, the pilot had to make his way to the nearest GPO telephone and ring back to base from there.

Philip Lucas summed up the doubt which existed in everybody's minds as the hair-raising series of tests continued: 'We did an awful lot of tests at Langley, trying to break off a tailplane. We kept on introducing modifications, strengthening the tailplane and the fuselage, but we did it with our tongues in our cheeks, simply because we knew that something had to be *seen* to be done. But every modification which we introduced was followed by yet another tailplane coming off. The flutter experts said it was not flutter but there were squadrons being formed, and morale was being affected by it'.

It took the best part of a year to overcome the problem, from late 1941 to late 1942. At the height of the crisis, Roland Beamont was detached from the RAF to return to Hawkers as a test pilot. He became involved at once in the efforts to recreate the conditions under which a Typhoon would lose its tail, and comments now: 'Each flight was a deliberate, callous, misuse of the aircraft, and at that point in my career I felt that it might be much safer to go back to fighting the Germans!

I could see we were getting up to the narrow end, and the chances were that the next thing you were asked to do would break the tail off. But, morally, you were absolutely committed to going on'.

He later wrote; 'It was as impressive an experience to dive this aircraft to 450mph indicated airspeed at 25,000 feet, where it shook with compressibility buffeting, and lost elevator effectiveness, as any one of our recent operations in 609 Squadron; but when I was invited to set up this condition while holding directional trim on rudder alone without trim bias and then, with feet taken off the rudder pedals, to cut the engine at full power on the ignition switches to produce a maximum possible yawing moment, I felt that this was becoming less than humorous. Yet the tail did not come off'.

RAE Farnborough were brought in to try to find a solution, and Robert Lickley was sent out from Hawkers at Kingston to the scene of every one of the crashes, all over the country, to make a minute inspection of the wreckage. One Typhoon which had shown signs of beginning to go through the flutter phase, but which had been brought out of it successfully, was grounded and transported to Farnborough, where it was put through flutter tests, then in their infancy. This particular incident came to light due to Hawker's methodical plan under which they posted their own mechanics to squadrons using Typhoons with instructions to keep their ears and eyes open for anything that might give a clue to the elusive trouble.

One of these mechanics, with a squadron based at Hurn, overheard a sergeant-pilot complaining that earlier in the day, when he had been flying and firing his guns, his whole machine had begun to shake. The mechanic rang up Philip Lucas in high excitement, and the aeroplane was pulled out of service and started on its way to Farnborough at once.

Once the fault had been cured, the Typhoon rapidly gained a reputation for being one of the toughest fighters ever made. Lucas said; 'No Tyhoon ever broke up as a result of rough handling by a pilot. Camm's basic all-metal design, with monococque rear fuselage and built-up box front fuselage, and with two-spar stressed-skin wings attached to the body by four bolts on each side, stood up to everything that the RAF's pilots could do to it, and particularly to the additional strain of high-speed operations at low level.'

At the hands of the Germans, both in the air and from the ground, the Typhoons accepted the sort of punishment which would have finished off other more lightly-constructed aeroplanes. Often they returned safely to their home airfields with sizeable pieces of airframe missing. Almost as dangerous as the hostile intentions of the enemy was the chance of striking ground obstacles during the low-level operations which proved to be the Typhoon's speciality. Flying in between flak ships, underneath high-tension cables, and in and out of wooded valleys, Typhoons frequently came into contact with the landscape; but because of their immense strength they enabled the pilot to fly back and tell the tale as he pulled the evidence — lengths of rigging and branches of trees — out of that monstrous radiator scoop.

Another Enigma- Compressibility

While the Hawker test pilots were trying to snap the tails off Typhoons, a further enigma was making itself known to both them and the fighter pilots in the early Typhoon squadrons. This was 'compressibility', a condition which caused the aircraft to become uncontrollable at the high speeds — in excess of Mach 0.75 which were being achieved in dives for the first time. Technically, the condition was produced when the airflow over the thick, unswept wing of the Typhoon was accelerated locally over aerofoils, fairings, bumps and uneven surfaces, and was compressed as the speed of sound was approached, breaking from laminar into turbulent flow patterns.

The results were dramatic, ranging from mild vibration to violent buffeting with changes of trim, to violent nose-up or nose-down pitching. The stick went dead, and all control was lost in the thin air at high altitude, the situation remaining unresolved until the Typhoon re-entered the denser air below 20,000 feet. Compressibility had been encountered as far back as the Tornado prototype. In an effort to come to grips with the problem, Hawkers stuck a series of small tufts of wool on the radiator fairing. The Tornado was then flown over a range of test conditions in close formation with a Hurricane whose pilot observed the behaviour of the tufts. He discovered that as buffet vibrations started, the wool, instead of streaming backwards, was in fact blowing forward, in the direction of flight.

The reason that the problem was not recognised within Hawkers during the early part of the programme was probably because the majority of test dives were started from 20,000 feet, at which height the conditions did not show. Odd reports started coming in from service pilots, but often the vivid descriptions of how the controls 'locked', only to return to their normal function in a mysterious manner, were dismissed as 'line-shooting', or the product of an over-excited imagination. A test pilot from the engine firm, Napier, experienced it when, after some tests at high altitude, he put his aircraft's nose down steeply to return to base in a hurry, as he had a social engagement that evening. Philip Lucas remembers him landing and describing how the controls had gone dead, a story that was dismissed by the manufacturers as 'nonsense'.

RAF pilots experienced the phenomenon when they began to encounter on patrols the new, high-speed Messerschmitt Me 210s. The only way to catch these fighters was to dive after them vertically, and this some members of No 1 Squadron, stationed at Acklington, did in August, 1942. Beginning their dives at 30,000 feet, their speeds probably approached 500mph as they roared down after the German aircraft, and during the chase they had the alarming experience of feeling their new machines go out of control. Like the others, they regained control below 20,000 feet.

Two of the 210s were shot down, and back at base the stories were taken more seriously, Lucas, who happened to be visiting Acklington at the time, questioned the pilots closely and noted what had happened. As a result, all pilots' notes for the Typhoon were amended. From that point, the men who had to fly the new aircraft at least knew what was happening when the buffeting began, and had the reassurance that if they left well alone, the condition would eventually solve itself when they reached a low enough altitude.

The Americans were experiencing the

same sort of problems at much the same time during high-speed dive tests which they were carrying out with the twin-engined, twin-boom P-38 Lightning fighter. A United States Army Air Force colonel, Cass Hough, had gained considerable fame from diving one of these machines out of control to what was claimed to be the speed of sound. Experts at RAE Farnborough tended to dismiss the claim, however, as they calculated that on that particular aeroplane at such velocities, total energy would have equalled total drag. They assumed that there must have been a fairly considerable error in the airspeed system.

Pilots on the Aerodynamics Flight at Farnborough were themselves experiencing compressibility as they explored the ultimate dive characteristics of Spitfires. Among the hazards which they faced were forced landings following the loss of propellers.

Roland Beamont encountered compressibility at its worst during the trials which he did for Hawkers to try to solve the mystery of the tail breakages: 'Charlie Dunn, the flight test engineer, briefed me that from a maximum power level at 30,000 feet, a push over into a near-vertical dive should enable us to reach about 450mph indicated at 20,000 feet.

'At 28,000 feet there was no clear space in sight for the required dive, but I levelled at 31,000 feet on top of a cirrus deck and pushed up the power to maximum boost and the phenomenal Sabre rpm limit of 3,750. As speed built up, a break occurred in the clouds to port, and at the bottom of a quite well-defined cloud shaft, a bend in the Thames near Eton could be seen.

'With instrumentation switches set for strain gauge recording, and initial flight conditions noted on the test pad, we peeled off to port, bringing the rpm back slightly as a margin against loss of propeller constant speed control in the dive, and rolling out into a near-vertical dive, trimmed with a slight residual push

force, again as a safety margin, this time against the anticipated nose-down effects of compressibility.

'At 27,000 feet the general noise and fuss were becoming impressive, with buffet vibration building up through the controls, seat and cockpit sides. Even the motor-car side windows were away at their natural frequency, and it was while observing this with interest that the situation developed suddenly. I was conscious of the controls stiffening up quite rapidly, of the port wing trying to drop, and of the aircraft becoming nose-heavy to the accompaniment of violent buffeting and a general feeling of insecurity. When beginning to bear back on the stick, to hold the dive angle from getting too steep, and holding off starboard aileron to maintain wings level, it was markedly apparent that these actions were ineffective.

'A full two-handed pull failed to reduce the dive angle at all, and we were now going downhill, and rolling to port, with maximum noise, buffet and general commotion, and with no conventional control of the situation.

'Here was the thing called compressibility, about which Philip Lucas had said: 'Whatever you do, don't trim it out of the dive', as the consequent trim reversal would probably overstress something severely. So I didn't and, with throttle right back, continued to ride the bucking and uncontrolled device down through 20,000 feet until we passed 15,000 feet where, as the Mach number dropped, the shock waves were supposed to subside and the elevator recover effectiveness.

'This indeed occurred and, with subsiding buffet, aileron effectiveness recovered first. Then the nose began to rise under my still heavy pull-force, until I was at last able to ease off the pressure and recover to a level attitude, still with the throttles closed, the indicated airspeed dropping back from 500mph and, impressively, the altimeter steadying at only 8,500 feet! I was no longer feeling the cold'.

They Flew Typhoons

Above: John Grandy (on the left) then a Group Captain (Chief of the Air Staff, April, 1967) talks as officer commanding RAF Duxford in 1942 to Wing Commander Dennis Gillam. Gillam was the leader of the first Typhoon wing to be formed.

Middle left: Among the aircraft insignia in the RAF Museum, Hendon, now lies the panel from the side of Wing Commander Beamont's Typhoon PR G bearing witness to his score as a train buster over France in 1942. The squadron badge is that of the 609 Auxiliary, formed from the Leeds – Bradford area, hence the white rose.

Bottom left: The panel *in situ* on Beamont's aircraft in 1943 with Beamont, then squadron commander, on the wing.

Far top left: Men of many nations flew Typhoons with the RAF. Flying Officer Polek of Poland. (Far centre left) Erik Haabjoern of Norway.

(Left) M. L. Van Neste, Charles de Moulin, Joseph Renier and Manu Geerts of Belgium. (Bottom left) The Argentinian 'Pancho' Pagnam and B. L. G. Foley, George Martin, J. D. McLaughlin and R. E. Bavington of Australia. (Below) Artie Ross of America.

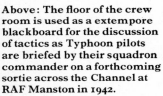

Above: The floor of the crew room is used as a extempore blackboard for the discussion of tactics as Typhoon pilots are briefed by their squadron commander on a forthcoming sortie across the Channel at RAF Manston in 1942.

Top middle right: Distinguished visitor; as the fame of the new Typhoons began to spread, the squadrons had to put on a 'show' for many of the 'top brass' who came down to see what they could really do. Here 609 entertain the Belgian Minister of War, M. Camille Gutt, at Duxford, 1942, flanking him on the wing with pilots from his own country. (Top far right) Another distinguished visitor was the Secretary of State for Air, Sir Archibald Sinclair, who visited 609 at Manston in 1943. On his right is Beamont while he is talking to Cheval Lallemant, a Belgian fighter pilot.

Middle right: Pilot Officer

Charles Detal, one of the group of Belgians who flew Typhoons with the RAF with 609 Squadron, became one of the foremost experts in ground attack (See page 71).

Bottom right: Whooping it up in the mess! Pilots of 609 Tyhhoon squadron in a relaxed mood off duty in their mess at Doone House, Manston in November, 1942, entertain a couple of visiting officers, including the CO of a whirlwind squadron (holding tankard).

Far right: Pilots of 609 Squadron had their own peculiar mascot while flying Typhoons, a goat named William, who found fame by being written up in the popular press, and who was rapidly 'promoted' through the RAF ranks. Here he gets pride of place, surrounded by officers serving with the squadron from six nations – Britain, Belgium, Canada, New Zealand, Norway and Poland.

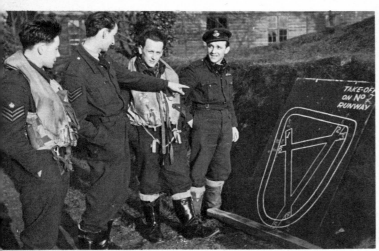

A FLT PILOTS		B FLT PILOTS	
SQUADRON FORMATION			
HARBJOERN	A	F/LT SMITH	O
ROBERTS	B	F/O VAN LIERDE DFC	L
PAYNE	H	F/O DAVIES	R Y T
SEERTS	H D	F/O REMIER	R Y T
NIBLETT		F/O BALDWIN DFC	T
WATTS		S/O SKETT	
DE MOULIN	K	F/O RAEHIL	
LESLIE	K L J	F/O JASPIS	
STARK	J	F/S BLANCO	X P V
BAVINTON	C	F/S McMANN	L
AITKEN-QUACK	C	Sgt DETAL	
HENRION		Sgt ZEGERS	48
WATELET		Sgt McLAUGHLIN	
BRYAN		Sgt ELLIS	
BERRY		Sgt FOLEY	S

10-7-43
OPS
NIL

LT COCKPIT READINESS

VICEABILITY		**A FLIGHT**		**B FLIGHT**		SERVICEABILITY		
U/S	REMARKS	**RED**		**BLUE**		A/C		REMARKS
U/S	NOT HELD	13·00 GEERTS	D	NIBLETT	F	A	/S	Not Held
U/S	NOT HELD	DE MOULIN	G	A-Q	H	U	/S	ENG. CHANGE
/S		**YELLOW**		**GREEN**		W/S	DI	
U/S	NOT HELD	14·00 LESLIE	O				/S	NOT HELD
/S		STARK	T				/S	NOT HELD
/S		**WHITE**		**BLACK**				NOT HELD
U/S	NOT HELD	15·00 ROBERTS	D			U/S		NOT HELD
/S	NOT HELD	WATELET	G			U/S		ENGINE CHANGE
U/S	NOT HELD					U/S		NOT HELD
U/S	NOT HELD					U/S		NOT HELD

TAKE-OFF ON NO 7 RUNWAY

Far top left: Dispersal, Manston, 1943; Typhoon pilots sit around waiting for the call from Operations to go into action. Some play cards, some read, some just reflect. Three dogs, squadron mascots, are in evidence. On the wall are the expected pin-ups, but the censor has expunged operational details written on the blackboard behind the stove, and has also cut out the number of the squadron – this was 609 – inscribed on a square of metal from a shot-down Ju 88 – hence the blank square on the wall.

Far middle left: Four Typhoon pilots gather at Manston airfield in the spring of 1943 around a blackboard on which the chosen direction of take – off for the day was displayed. All from 609 Squadron, they are, left to right, Flight Sergeant Baker, Sergeant Leslie, Pilot Officer Polek, and Flying Officer Van Lierde.

Left: Achtung! Typhoon! Although they are wearing what looks like German Iron Crosses, these pilots are in fact from 181 Squadron, flying Typhoons. It was in March, 1943, at Cranfield, at the beginning of 'Exercize Spartan', designed to test the Allied forces for the invasion of Europe which took place 15 months later. 83 Group including 181, were told off to act as the 'enemy', presumably because of the Typhoon's resemblance to the Focke Wulf Fw 190, and to make low – level attacks on airfields in Britain defended by Spitfires and Hurricanes. The squadron commanding officer, Squadron Leader Crowley-Milling, (right briefing his pilots) entered into the spirit of the thing and had his men decked out in Iron Crosses – made out of wood!

Bottom left: Gloom in the squadron operations room on July 10, 1943, as 609 Squadron flight commander Erik Haabjoern surveys a depressing state board which shows only four Typhoons serviceable, and no operations.

Below: Typhoon pilots excitedly describe their experiences after returning to their base at Lympne in October, 1943, from an operation over the continent.

Versus the Fw 190s

Scenes showing a typical Typhoon squadron scramble at RAF Manston, 1943. (Below) The aircraft leave their dispersals and are already loosely forming up. (Bottom) They taxi out on to airfield.

Below right: Eight Typhoons, showing their black and white underwing stripes painted to avoid confusion from the ground with the Focke Wulf 190, fly by in the classic 'finger four' fighter formation. This was a demonstration at Tangmere in the summer of 1943, and the aircraft were much closer together than they would have been in 'Search Formation' on operations. The finger four formation allowed each pilot to look across and watch the tails of his wingmen.

The RAF gave the Typhoon the primary task of acting as an interceptor of the Focke-Wulf 190s which, in 1942, were infiltrating singly or in pairs at low level across the south coast of England, dropping bombs on and straffing military and non-military objectives. The raids had a nuisance value against the British war effort, sending workers all too frequently from their benches for shelter as the alert sounded, and generally causing a lowering of the morale of the civilian population.

Fw 190s were operating in the worst-possible weather conditions and, due to their superior speed, the RAF's Spitfires were having little success in seeking them out and destroying them. Thrown in against them in the autumn of 1942, the Typhoons began at once to record successes and, at the same time, to refurbish their battered reputation.

Standing patrols were flown from dawn to dusk over the middle of the Channel in all weathers. The 'kills' recorded against the 190s had, however,

to be balanced against the losses of Typhoons through the still-brittle state of the Sabre engine. Few Typhoon pilots survived a ditching in the winter sea.

The showing which the Typhoons were making against the modern fighter-bombers which the Germans had in their armoury at that time impressed the RAF high command and went a long way towards saving the type from any further cuts in production or suggestions of cancellation. It also made the hierarchy more receptive to (at the time) radical suggestions from Beamont that, using the Typhoon, the war should be taken into the enemy's territory with a vengeance.

Spitfires and Hurricanes had been flying for some time what were known as *Rhubarbs* — search-and-destroy sorties into France — but Beamont realized the increased potential of the new aircraft, with its speed, ruggedness, heavy armament, and stability as a firing platform, in such operations.

He put up the idea to a slightly-

surprised AOC of No 11 Group, and was within certain limits, given a free hand to go ahead and attack the enemy wherever he and his squadron — 609 — could find them, the projected targets ranging from shipping in the Channel, through trains, road transport, military formations, gun emplacements, radar stations, and air-fields, to aircraft on the ground and in the air.

The only proviso that was made to the relatively free hand which Beamont received was that this offensive activity should not interfere with the Channel-patrol brief which had been given to the Typhoons, it being pointed out that because of the recurrent unserviceability problems the squadron had been reduced to only six aircraft available out of 22 on many occasions.

Rhubarbs with Typhoons fell into two main categories — those in pairs across the Channel during daytime, usually in bad weather, and those carried out with single aircraft at night by the light of the moon. The suggestion by Beamont that

Typhoons should be used in the latter role caused raised eyebrows at squadron level, as he humorously recorded later: 'There was still a feeling that 609 was a day squadron, and that air fighting stopped between sundown and dawn, during which period you were on your own and in the 'local'. And yet here was a crazy squadron commander wanting to go out after dark and fight the war single-handed. This attitude lasted for three days, and then I asked who wanted to come along. We had a flight commander's benefit for a few days, and then we had a queue of chaps volunteering for night raids, and we used to pick and choose who we wanted to do it. I had to introduce a high standard of night training, and make them go on night cross-country exercises in Britain first.'

November 17, 1942, saw the first daytime *Rhubarb,* and the following night the first night solo, by Beamont who attacked trains in the area of the Somme. It took a great deal of dedicated courage at that time for 609's pilots to climb into the still highly-suspect Typhoon and take off at night un-accompanied, with thoughts that your engine could die on you at any moment, over hostile territory, and with further thoughts that you didn't have to do it, and that you could have been back in the mess with a pint of beer in your hand. But these Typhoon sorties proved to be one of the pivots on which the war, began to swing round and became offensive rather than defensive from Britain's point of view. Their introduction, during late 1942, marked an important mile-stone in the changing fortunes of war.

By the middle of 1943, the sweeps were penetrating further and further into occupied Europe, taking in large sections of northern France, Belgium and Holland. Railway engines were being put out of action at the rate of around 150 a month, while one Typhoon pilot flew back to base with a 'bag' which included a tug, an R-boat and two barges. 609 Squadron alone were credited with putting over 100 locos out of action in a three-month period. At the same time, the standing-patrol responsibility was met, and 609 shot down 14 Fw 190s.

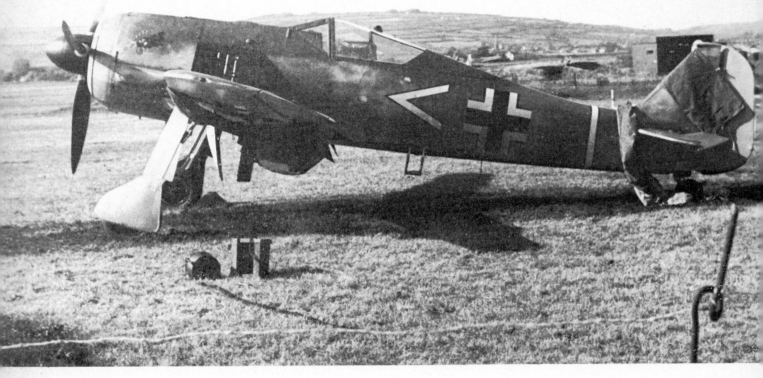

Above: Unscheduled visitors;
Britain was made a 'present'
of one of Germany's new
Focke Wulf Fw 190 fighters
– arch rivals of the Typhoon
in combat – when the pilot
force-landed the aircraft in
perfect condition at Pembrey,
Wales, in 1942. Beamont later
test flew the 190 from
Farnborough and assessed
its capabilities. (Below) The
following year a second 190
fell unexpectedly into British
hands when a German pilot
(on the left) landed in error at
night at Manston, thinking it
was his base in northern
France. He is pictured here
the morning after with the
station Intelligence Officer
(centre) and Johnny Wells of
609 Squadron. In the doorway
stand armed guards.

Left: Close-up of the port wheel and flap mechanism of a Typhoon. Parked in the background and just visible under the wing is a Tiger Moth representing an earlier era of aviation.

Above: Servicing in the field; ground crew have stripped this Typhoon down drastically while they work on it. Three aircraftmen are busy underneath, while a fourth works on the engine.

All of the cowling covering the Sabre has been removed, as have most of the panels surrounding the cockpit.

Below: A fine war-time drawing of five Typhoons in a typical setting – at low level over the Channel just off the white cliffs on patrol awaiting the arrival of hit-and-run Focke Wulf Fw 190 raiders.

The fitting of the first bomb racks on the Typhoons of 609 at Manston in 1943 brought out the official Air Ministry photographers for some public relations footage. (Right) A Belgian pilot Mony Van Lierde is surrounded by an admiring group of WAAFs as Wings for Victory stamps are stuck all over the 500-pounder under the wing. (Far right) He receives a carefully-staged end-off as he taxis away. The following year, Van Lierde became a top scorer against flying bombs, shooting down 52 in Tempests.

Below right: Under the shadow of the twin cannons of a Typhoon, in a carefully-posed wartime propaganda shot, a pilot makes up the squadron scoreboard, while the squadron commander, a Norwegian, carefully blots out the tell-tale number with his hand. The squadron was No 56, the first to receive the new fighter.

Far bottom right: The camera gun record taken from the aircraft of Pilot Officer C. Detal of 609 Squadron, during the strafing of a German airfield to the south of Paris. The three photographs show a Junkers Ju 88 bomber being struck by his fire and then collapsing, badly damaged, on to its port wing.

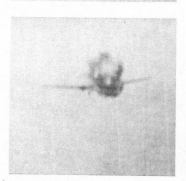

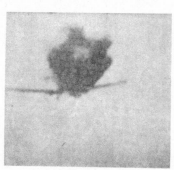

On the rampage over northern France, the Low Countries and the North Sea and Channel, Typhoons caused untold damage to German military equipment, the occupied railways, and shipping, while giving heart to those who were living under Nazi domination. (Right) These camera gun shots show a Belgian Typhoon pilot shooting down a Junkers Ju 52 transport. (Middle right) A Ju 88 bomber being peppered on the ground (a crewman can be seen making his escape under the fuselage) and (Below) Luftwaffe aircraft being shot up while on their airfields. (Bottom middle right) Trains being 'brewed up' by Typhoon cannon fire. (Far bottom right) Canal shipping under fire. (Far right) Ships damaged or sunk at Lubeck in the final days of the war during the drive into Europe.

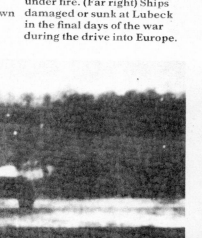

Typhoon Toughness

Typhoons were not always on the giving end, but because of their immensely strong construction, they were often able to return home with damage which would have finished off other fighter types. (Top left) Pilot Officer Stark stands before his battered aircraft, which has gaping holes in the nose, and badly dented air scoop and spinner, after being hit by flak. (Below left) Diverting from Manston after a night intruder sortie in 1943, the pilot cartwheeled on landing this Typhoon at Bradwell Bay – but got out alive. (Below) Roland Beamont, as a young squadron commander, crash-landed on the cliffs at Dover after the Sabre engine of his Typhoon had died on him, and continued to run the squadron from his hospital bed. (Bottom) Flight Lieut Erik Haaboern, a Norwegian, landed his Typhoon in this condition at Manston after being struck during an anti-shipping patrol – and lived to pose for the photographer. (Top right) A present from Hitler; another Typhoon brought back with this unexploded anti-aircraft cannon shell in the leading edge of its wing. (Bottom right) Mike Brian surveys the sky through a hole in his starboard wing after a shipping strike among the Dutch islands.

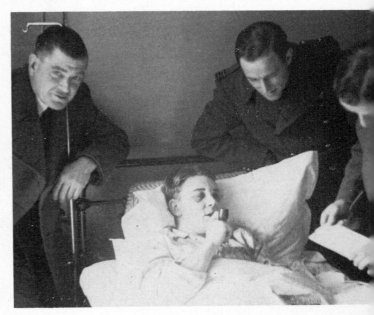

Left: Pilot Officer John Skett brough his machine back with anti-aircraft fragments riddling the tail.

Below: Demonstrating beyond any doubt the immense toughness of construction of the Typhoon, the pilot emerged unscathed from this disastarous crash at New Romney, Kent, in August, 1943. It happened as a squadron came into land. The pilot saw he was coming too close to the Tyhpoon in front, and pushed his nose up to lose speed. In doing so, he stalled, cartwheeled across the airfield, tearing off a wing, the tail and the engine, and finishing up on his back, still strapped into the cockpit, from which he was assisted with no more than shock and a few bruises.

Right: This forced landing by a Typhoon of 609 Squadron at RAF Biggin Hill in October, 1942, was graphically illustrated due to the fact that by a coincidence a film was being made on the airfield at the time by the Boulting brothers. They filmed the belly landing after the Typhoon pilot, Flying Officer Roy Payne had radioed to say that he was unable to get his wheels down. The story had a happy ending, as Payne stepped out unhurt, and the Typhoon's main damage was confined to a badly bent propeller. (Payne was lost in action later in the year.)

The 'Bomphoons' Arrive

Air Marshal Denis Crowley-Milling recalled that in September, 1942, he formed the first Typhoon-bomber squadron, No 181. It was a brand-new unit, and was followed shortly by two others, Nos 182 and 183. Later, the Typhoons in this new role became known in the newspapers as 'Bomphoons', but this was not a title which was current when the squadrons were first established.

The practice of using World War II fighters in the bombing role had been tried early in 1942 with Hurricanes. Early attempts to have these aircraft flying over targets in the horizontal plane

to drop their bombs had proved unsuccessful, as there was no certainty about where the weapons would land. The Hurricanes were then turned into dive-bombers and recorded much greater accuracy.

Air Marshal Crowley-Milling told how, later: 'We practised with the Typhoons against derelict ship targets in the Wash, and then developed operations against German fighter bases in France and the low countries. We used to time our approach to coincide with the return of the big United States Army Air Force B-17 daylight raids, so that we arrived as the German fighters which had been up to intercept them were breaking away, short of fuel and ammunition, and landing back at their airfields. The squadron would cross the Channel at nought feet to get under the German radar, climbing to around 10,000 feet at the French coast. We would then go straight in to places like Caen, Abbeville, St Omer, Triqueville, and Poix, diving from 10,000 feet and letting the bombs go at around 5,000 to 6,000 feet, so keeping clear of the light flak.

'As you dived down, you could look behind and see the heavy flak bursting to the rear. We developed a pretty good accuracy; on one occasion one of our bombs actually burst under an enemy aircraft as it was touching down. The whole essence of the operation was to hit and then get out fast; it did not do to hang around. If you were jumped by fighters, you jettisoned the bombs, but this seldom happened. On the approach to a target the Typhoon, being such a splendid aircraft, could cruise at nearly 300mph low-down without little ill-effects on its performance from the load hanging under its wings.

'Airfields were not the Typhoon-bombers' only targets. We also attacked industrial centres such as steel works, and shipping off the Dutch coast. The ships were generally heavily-defended with flak, and the usual practice was to attack in pairs with only the number two aircraft carrying bombs. The leader of each pair would fire his guns to keep down the flak, preparing for the approach of the bomber.

Far left: Denis Crowley Milling, then a Squadron Leader, today an Air Marshal, poses in 1943 in the cockpit of his 'Bomphoon' Typhoon fighter-bomber. The 'Austin 7' type door, which together with the push-up hood, were so disliked by pilots can be clearly seen, although by this stage of the war the metal fairing behind the cockpit had been replaced by clear-view Perspex.

Far bottom left: One of 181 Squadron's 'Bomphoons' runs up its Sabre at Duxford in 1943 producing two typical visual reactions to its clamour, which one engine fitter described as reminscent of the tearing of a huge strip of calico – the engine exhausts stream smoke, and the officer in the foreground claps his hands over his ears.

Left: Armourers winch a 500 lb bomb into place under the wing of a Typhoon. One man works the handle on either side, a third steadies the bomb at the rear. The panels giving access to the cannon feed can be seen folded open on top of the wing. Picture taken in May, 1943.

Bombing up the Typhoon. (far top left) In the first picture the bombs, 500-pounders, arrive on a series of trolleys towed by a tractor driven by a WAAF, while the armourers move in. (Top middle) Part of the bomb mounting under the wing of the aircraft is removed and a portable winch is inserted. The trolley is pushed underneath, and wires hooked round the bomb. (Top) Steadied by the corporal at the front, the bomb is carefully winched upwards so that its attachment mates with a hook in the mounting. (Above middle) The attachment made, the winch panel is screwed back into the mounting, and the wire which arms the bomb as it falls is fastened to the centre of the tail fin. (Above) The final operation; the crutches which steady the bomb on its mounting are screwed up – but not too tightly, or the bomb would stick up under the aircraft instead of releasing. These pictures were taken at Tangmere in the summer of 1943 in a carefully-staged Air Ministry exercize to publicize the formation of the first Typhoon-bomber squadron, No 181. (Left) In the last picture the camera party can be seen assembling their gear (on the right) while the ground crew take a breather and find it all a bit of a joke.

'Rhubarbs' by Day and Night

Rhubarbs by both day and night are graphically described by Beamont:

By day, the method was for two aircraft to fly to the planned target area at zero feet across the Channel to avoid radar detection, and then to go into a steep climb when sighting the enemy coast, crossing above 2,000 feet to avoid light flak, and then back down to 200-300 feet from about ten miles inland to search for targets.

When defensive fire was encountered, as it generally was, we would really get down between the trees and behind the farmhouses, out of the line of fire. During the winter period, in which the squadron logged successful attacks on more than 100 goods trains and many other targets, including aircraft, army vehicles and naval vessels, we had no pilot killed by ground fire, although many aircraft were hit.

Night tactics were different. We operated as single aircraft by moonlight and cruised over France at 10,000 feet, holding this height until descending on course and time from a prominent landmark in the target area. We found that by moonlight the best height for target search was about 1,500 feet. Above this one could not pick out detail, and much below it one could not see far enough ahead.

This meant that you were exposed to searchlights and light flak; but with good briefing from the Intelligence Section we had a fair idea of where these were and how best to approach them. When suddenly engaged by the weaving chains of tracer from 40mm guns, or

enveloped at short range in searchlight glare, the wrong thing proved to be to try and climb out of it. The right thing was to dive at full power for the deck, as low as you could get, in view of the inability to see the ground or much of your instruments in the glare.

As this action developed, the enemy took urgent steps to increase the quantity and quality of the gun defences of trains, and we began to encounter heavy fire from multiple machine-gun and 23mm cannon turrets. But these did not affect the method of attack, which was to stop the train and 'brew up' the engine to create steam identification of the target which could then be seen for miles in the moonlight and, on the second attack, to engage the flak car, which generally revealed itself as soon as one opened fire.

The long effective range of our 20mm Hispano cannon was an important feature of these attacks, as we could fire a short burst from about 1,000 yards on the way in, see the high-explosive shells explode and illuminate the train and, if necessary, correct aim to bring the main burst on the target. The speeds used at night were 250-300mph so as to keep the target in sight; but in daylight 350-400mph was normal to get in and out as quickly as possible. Later, with the Tempest, higher speeds were possible; but except for cases of very heavily defended targets the lower speeds were still used to permit reasonable time for vision of the target.

It is of interest to note that in the combat conditions of wars fought more recently, weapons delivery in closely-confined country or limited weather was still carried out mainly in the 400-500 knot speed bracket, and that the fixed gun is still a significantly-useful weapon, due to its pinpoint accuracy.

During 1943, the Typhoon was used widely for ground attack with guns, low-level air defence, as a long-range bomber-destroyer, and in its ultimate role of ground attack with bombs and rocket projectiles. After coming close to cancellation in 1942 for technical reasons and because of the Spitfire lobby, it had by early 1944 equipped the ground-attack wings of the Second Tactical Air Force which were to have a major effect on the course of the subsequent ground battle in France and Germany.

A Potent Weapon of Attack

Armament of the Typhoon became progressively heavier as its short but vivid career progressed and the RAF realised fully what a potent weapon of attack they had in this aircraft. Only a few of the earlier machines were fitted with 12 machine-guns, these Mark IA versions soon giving way to the IB, with four 20mm cannons. These were first in action during the Dieppe raid of August 19, 1942, and the first recorded 'kill' by the new fighter was credited to 266 Rhodesian squadron, whose pilots shot down a Junkers Ju 88 reconnaissance aircraft over the North Sea ten days earlier.

Hurricanes had been fitted with two 250lb bombs under their wings and were having some success against enemy shipping in the Channel. It was a natural follow-on to treat the stronger, more powerful Typhoon in a similar fashion. By the end of 1942 Nos 175, 181 and 245 Squadrons began to be converted into fighter-bombers, the 'Bomphoons'.

It was soon realised that the Typhoon could do far more than carry 500lb of bombs, so the load was steadily increased, first to 1,000lb, and then to 2,000lb. But the Typhoon really came into its own as an offensive weapons system when it was mated with rocket projectiles. This conversion took place in 1943 during the long run-up to the D-Day landings in June of the following year. Although the powers-that-be could appreciate the punch that Typhoons so equipped would wield, to the fighter pilot in the field, the treating of his Typhoon — which by now he was beginning to cherish rather than hate —

as a glorified Christmas tree was verging on sacrilege.

Nevertheless, shipping up and down the channel, and around the Dutch islands, soon began to feel the effect of the Bomphoons, and the enemy were forced to make the defences of the accompanying flak vessels stronger and stronger. A graphic description of one such attack is provided by Seymour 'Buck' Feldman, an American who joined the RAF in November, 1941, and was posted to No 3 Squadron late in 1942 as they were phasing out Hurricanes in favour of the Typhoon.

'The bombs were fitted with a three-second delay so that they would go off below the waterline. It was known as skip-bombing, and if you were really skilful at it, you could bounce your bomb off the water before it hit the ship. The ships were heavily defended, and it was necessary to fly into the cone of flak while attacking. One 3 Squadron pilot, Flight Sergeant McCook, a New Zealander, actually struck the water during an attack. The rest of us thought he had been lost, as he disappeared in an enormous cloud of spray; but he flew back to base complaining of vibration, and was found to have bent the ends of his propeller blades through 90 degrees.'

Squadrons whose Typhoons were fitted with rockets were sent to armament practice camps in Britain. There they practised the new flying and firing techniques which, when successfully deployed, were going to play such a major role in the D-Day invasion, and in the later drive through northern Europe. The pilots were taught to dive steadily at angles of 30 and then 60 degrees. An unflinching aim was essential, although the crews quickly realized that without the ability to 'jink' as they approached their target, they were sitting ducks for any ground gunner with nerve enough to stay at his post and continue squeezing the trigger.

The main objection, however, continued to be that all the ironmongery which was being hung on the Typhoon was destroying its capability as a successful low-level fighter. Each rocket weighed 60lb, and the load for each

The terrible destructive power of the rocket-firing Typhoon is demonstrated by this picture, taken soon after D-day, 1944, of Rommel's headquarters in northern France. The chateau was attacked by 609 Squadron just before the invasion, but the German commanders had just left the building.

aircraft was quickly increased from eight to 12. This was in addition to the four Hispano cannon, which the rocket Typhoons continued to carry. As Lieutenant Colonel Raymond Lallemant, the distinguished Belgian Typhoon pilot, wrote later in his book *Rendezvous With Fate* (Macdonald); 'As soon as the rockets were slung aboard their rails, the Typhoon, already weighed down with its armour-plating, sagged under the yoke and became little more than a flat iron, weakened in defence both against flak and enemy fighters.'

But the Typhoon was a good enough aeroplane to rise above such fears. With its rockets and its four cannon, each of which fired at the rate of 650 shells a minute — or 11 a second — with the magazines exhausted after 15 seconds — it had been turned into a fearsome weapon of war. This was proved time and time again, not only in the big set-piece battles, but in numerous small, individual operations on selected targets.

Perhaps the most sensational of those was the attack by 609 and 198 Squadrons on Rommel's headquarters in a chateau on the Cherbourg peninsula, on the eve of D-Day. Rommel, in charge of the German defences against the coming invasion, had left the chateau shortly before the Typhoons swept in. Pictures of the devastation to the house taken after the Allied landing show its facade full of gaping holes. Had the German general been in residence at the time, his chances of survival would have been slight.

The meeting was merely delayed, for a few weeks later Typhoons of 193 Sqdn attacked his staff car, wounding him. That was in July, 1944, and in October the same year Typhoons of 193, 197, 257, 263 and 266 Squadrons struck a further blow against the German army high command when they raided the headquarters of the 15th army at Dordrecht with 500lb and 1,000lb bombs, killing over 70 staff officers.

These were all carefully-planned operations, but the Typhoon attack which remains most memorable was carried out without any official premeditation, and against the desires of the

"Boys, meet Mr. Jones. He flies a Rocket-Typhoon."

RAF. This was when a Belgian pilot from 609 Squadron on a *Rhubarb* from Manston made a single-handed raid on Gestapo headquarters in Brussels, situated in a building in the Avenue de Louise. Flight Lieutenant Baron Jean de Selys Longchamps, a former Belgian cavalry officer, chose to make the attack as a gesture of contempt against the nation which had occupied his country, and as an encouragement for his countrymen living in the oppressed capital city.

According to reports which appeared in the British newspapers soon afterwards, de Selys Longchamps fooled the Germans in the headquarters into rushing to the windows by flying his machine so that they though it was going to crash. Using his cannon, he then shot in the upper and lower windows. Pulling away, he opened the side window of the cockpit and threw out Belgian and British flags. It was discovered later by the Allies that 30 Gestapo had been killed in the raid, but that among them was one British secret agent in whose pocket was found a list of names which led to the arrest of a hundred others.

This gem of a cartoon, by courtesy of Mr D. Helmore, who was a Typhoon pilot with 137 Squadron during the drive through Germany and then into Denmark, illustrates the impact that the rocket attacks had on morale among the retreating German troops. It was taken from a Canadian forces newspaper in January, 1945.

93

In this series of pictures, taken on July 9, 1944, a month after the Allies had landed in Europe, the process of loading up Typhoons with rockets is clearly illustrated. (Right) Armourers are about to clip the rockets on to the underwing rails – but the rockets are only of the practice variety, and have heads made of concrete. (Far right) Without doubt, the real thing; the 60 lb high-explosive heads are attached to the body, with the fins at the top. (Below) Loaded on to trolleys the projectiles are taken out to dispersal; the port wing of the Typhoon is already armed with its quota of four RPs, and the starboard wing is about to be similarly serviced. (Below right) The clips holding the projectiles slide gently down the rails, carefully guided by two ground crew. A third armourer on the wing attends to the ammunition for the 20 mm cannon.

Right: On a visit to an RAF station on May 5, 1944, King George VI is shown a Typhoon armed with rocket projectiles ready for softening-up operations before the invasion of Europe, then a month away. Bags of bull was the order of the day, even on an operational station, for the visit of His Majesty, and the Typhoon and its weapons appear to have been given a going-over with a dose of elbow grease.

Far right: Tough-going into Europe; it was hot work arming Typhoons in July, 1944, as the invasion progressed. Here a groundcrew member, stripped to the waist, but wearing his tin helmet, carries a 60 lb rocket projectile out to a waiting fighter on an advance airfield just behind the front line.

Below: All the immense power packed into the armament of the rocket-firing Typhoon is summed up in this remarkable shot which freezes all four projectiles a split second after they have left the underwing rails. The target in this attack in September, 1944, is a tug off the coast of Holland. The splashes in the water are cannon shells fired with the dual objectives of getting the anti-aircraft gunners' heads down so that the Typhoon had an uninterrupted run in, and as ranging shots for the rockets.

Below right: By February, 1945, the power of the Typhoon as an assault aircraft was being further strengthened with the arrival in Europe of anti-personnel bombs. The canister contains 26 single 20 lb weapons of this sort, one canister being carried under each wing. They were dropped in support of Allied ground forces during the Cleve offensive. In the picture armourers are fitting the nose and tail units on to the canister.

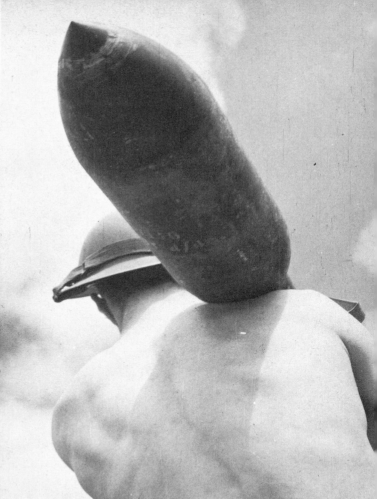

Top left: In Holland in January, 1945, fitters had to contend with sub-zero temperatures as they worked on the aircraft. Corporal E. Sadley, of Henley-on-Thames, and Leading Aircraftman G. A. Doust, of Stratford-on-Avon, work on a Typhoon parked on the edge of a wood. They have the engine cowlings, the spinner, and a section of wing leading edge removed – but despite the snow, gloves are not in evidence.

Middle left: Even in August 1944, two months after the invasion, conditions in Normandy could be treacherous; here ground crew and pilots work together to push a bogged-down Typhoon out of trouble. (Bottom left) A Typhoon, armed with two 1,000 lb bombs, ploughs through a watersplash on its way to take-off from Eindhoven airfield in February, 1945; the operation was against a railway target just behind the German front line in an effort to prevent reinforcements massing against a British-Canadian advance.

Left: Typhoons and Tempest Vs 'liberated' Denmark from the Germans on May 9, 1945, being the first Allied aircraft, with Spitfire 14s from 41 Squadron, to land at Kastrup airport, Copenhagen. The Typhoons were from 137 Squadron and the Tempests from 486 Squadron, all three squadrons forming 125 Wing. This picture of 137 Squadron was taken the following month at Kastrup, and under the starboard wing of the Typhoon around which the pilots are grouped can be seen an Me 109 of the defeated Luftwaffe. The RAF squadron personnel were greeted with wild enthusiasm by the liberated Danes and such were the celebrations that very little flying was accomplished during the following fortnight. The RAF were greeted at Kastrup by the Danish 'underground' freedom movement who were busy rounding up collaborators in the city. For several days, until they agreed to be confined to barracks, the German armed forces walked the streets and rubbed shoulders with the newly-arrived RAF. Immediately after the ceasefire in Germany, pilots of 137 Squadron found in a siding one of the German flak trains, complete with its crew, who boasted that they had shot down around 400 Allied aircraft. The pilots counted 196 anti-aircraft guns on the train, not one of them under 37mm calibre.

Right: Typhoons mass on one of the former homes of the Luftwaffe which, by May, 1945, had become property of the Allies. This is the airfield at Luneberg, with damaged hangars visible in the background. In the foreground are stacked hundreds of rocket projectiles ready for further attacks on the fleeing Germans. But this scene, taken on May 2, was soon to become peaceful, for three days later, on May 5, the general order went out from Allied headquarters for the shooting to stop. The Germans had surrendered, and the warlike growl of the Typhoons and the Tempests died away for the final time.

Bottom right: This was a sight which very soon became impossible to repeat, as 35 Typhoons take part in a fly-past on May 24, 1945, 19 days after the end of hostilities in Europe. They are followed in the distance by a further large group. Typhoons were rapidly replaced in the squadrons by Tempests, and by the end of the following year there were very few flying examples remaining.

The last of a long line of Typhoons was this aircraft, seen on the tarmac at the Gloster airfield at Brockworth in 1945 with its test pilot. A total of 3,330 Typhoons were built, almost all by Gloster, and at the period at which this picture was taken, brand-new aircraft were coming off the production line to be dismantled on the other side of the airfield.

Enter the Tempest

Camm had first considered a successor to the Typhoon when that aircraft was on its flight trials in 1940 and the snags in its basic design began to show up. By February, 1941, talks between him and the Director of Technical Development were taking place, at which Camm was able to display a design study for a developed Typhoon which used a wing with a semi-elliptical plan more akin to that of the Spitfire and, more important in view of the Typhoon's troubles with compressibility, a wing which was five inches thinner at the root.

The design at that time was known as the Typhoon II. Permission to go ahead was given to Hawkers in March, 1941 under Air Ministry specification F 10/41. On November 18 that year a contract was placed for two prototypes of a machine which was to be, as one contemporary writer put it, 'a Typhoon with the bugs out.' What emerged were three main variants, each of which was so different in design from the Typhoon that a new name was found — the Tempest. They were the Tempest I, with an uprated Sabre engine, a four-bladed propeller, and a very clean layout, with the radiators taken away from the distinctive bulky chin of the Typhoon and incorporated in the wing-root leading-edge; the Tempest II, with a Centaurus sleeve-valve radial engine; and the Tempest V, with the uprated Sabre, a longer nose, and an extended radiator back in the traditional position under the nose.

Lucas made the first flight in the prototype Mark V on September 2, 1942, the Mark I making its maiden flight on February 24, 1943. The Hawker test pilots carrying out trials of the new aircraft at Langley felt at once that they had in their hands a livelier, more precise, and more aggressive fighter than the Typhoon. The impressive strides forward in performance embodied in the Tempest can be seen by the fact that by the end of 1943 Bill Humble, the Hawker senior experimental test pilot, and Beamont, back with the company for a second spell of development flying, were in performance tests alternately exceeding the world speed record of 464mph which had been set in 1939 by a German in a Messerschmitt.

A top speed in level flight of 472mph was eventually attained — a very high performance for a propeller-driven aircraft at that stage of aviation development; but this potential of the Tempest was never realized in combat, as the sleek Mark I version was passed over in favour of the Mark V, with its lower performance, when the final configuration was selected.

Two major considerations dictated this choice. These were, the limited development of the Sabre IV engine, and fears within the Air Staff that the Tempest I radiators would be highly vulnerable to ground fire as they were spread out along the underside of the wing roots. Delays in the engine development programme and in perfecting the new radiator layout had already resulted in the Mark V flying before the Mark I, and production contracts were later firmed up on the former version. A further problem with the Mark I design was that the new, thinner wing had too little room left for fuel tanks after it had accommodated the radiators.

The first Tempest V in the first batch of 100 on order was flown by Humble from Langley on June 21, 1943. These early aircraft were armed with long Mark II Hispano cannon, but the Tempest V Series II which followed was equipped with shorter Hispano Mark V guns buried inside the wings, so enhancing the performance of the aeroplane. Beamont summed up his early experience with the new fighter-bomber as follows: 'In the Tempest we had a direct successor to the Typhoon with most of the criticised aspects of the latter either eliminated, or much improved.

'Each flight brought greater enjoyment of and confidence in the crisp ailerons, firm though responsive elevator, good directional stability and damping giving high promise of superior gun — aiming capability, exhilerating performance and, with all this, magnificent combat vision, with windscreen forward frame members thinned down to a bare minimum, and superb unobstructed vision aft of the windscreen arch through a fully — transparent sliding canopy.

'On every convenient occasion on the way back from tests I would zoom-climb, wing-over and rack the Tempests around in stall-boundary turns, simulating combat, looking over my shoulder down the fuselage and under my tailplane for the first time in my experience. What a fighter this would have made for the Battle of Britain, but what a fighter it was going to make for the invasion!

Commanded by Beamont, the first Tempest wing was formed at Newchurch, Kent, in April, 1944, with Nos 3 and 486 Squadrons being equipped first, followed, in July, by 56 Squadron. The Tempests were in business, but behind the scenes troubles continued to rumble.

Three Tempest squadrons should have been formed by D-Day, June 4, but the pace of production was slowed by a strike in the Hawker assembly shops following dissatisfaction over levels of pay, which had dropped temporarily when Hurricane quantity production had given way to tooling up for the new fighter. The dispute only came to public notice when, during a visit by the press to see D-Day preparations, Beamont was asked why there were only two squadrons. He replied, bluntly, that it was because of a strike, and his remark produced 'rockets' from both the Air Ministry and Hawkers. Beamont said later: 'It said much for the tolerance of our government organization even in wartime that people in the defence industry could strike — and get away with it.'

Boscombe Down, the government establishment which evaluates all new aircraft for the RAF, had several reservations about the Tempest which, had they not been modified could have had a serious effect on the aircraft's career. Philip Lucas recalls that when the prototype went there it was approved with a very good report, on the basis of which it was put into production. But by the time the first production machine was sent to Boscombe for trials, a different set of service test pilots had taken over and these sent a report back through headquarters to Hawkers at Langley that Tempests were not, in their view, fit for operational use until a long list of modifications had been carried out.

None of these mods were serious, and it would have been quite normal to do them in peacetime. But if they had been done at that time it would have meant, in the estimation of Lucas, putting back the introduction of Tempests by nine months to a year. 'We all went through the roof over that. There was an awful lot of behind-the-scenes lobbying with the operational people, and eventually an enormous meeting in London between Boscombe Down, Hawkers and the Ministry, at which the Boscombe report was overruled. Very soon after that the flying bomb attacks were to begin, against which the Tempests proved invaluable.'

Although they had none of the major snags of the early Typhoons, the early Tempests were certainly not faultless, as the pilots in the first squadrons to receive them soon found. Buck Feldman recalls: 'Most pilots liked the Tempest, as it was the aircraft they were used to, while having performance improvements. Initially, however, there were problems with failure of a seal in the constant-speed propeller hydraulics. These tended

Three of the men who played a vital role in the birth of the Typhoon – Tempest series, from left to right, Sydney Camm, designer of the aircraft, Mr A. Burke, assistant managing director of Napiers, manufacturers of the Sabre engine, and Mr H. K. Jones, managing director of Hawkers. They are inspecting the Tempest I prototype which dispensed with the big chin air scoop in favour of ducted radiators along the wing leading edges. This version did not go into production.

The Tempest I, despite its classification, flew after the Tempest V, the delay being mainly due to development problems with the Sabre IV engine. It had its radiators along the wing leading edges, but this configuration produced objections from the Air Ministry, who considered them vulnerable to ground fire. The version was cancelled after there had been further engine-development snags.

to blow under pressure, causing the propeller to run away and resulting in some exciting effects, with bits of metal coming out through the exhaust ports as things broke up inside. The problem was solved by backing the seal with copper.

'The engine also overheated badly and, as the camera was mounted in the lip of the engine intake, the emulsion on the films would run. There was also engine vibration, and the result was that very few good films were taken of early Tempest operations. Later on, the camera was moved to a position on the wing.

'I was a personal victim of these faults when I took one of the early Tempests up from the squadron at Bradwell Bay after the riggers and armourers had checked it so that I could test-fire the guns. I was just going out over the Channel when the propeller ran away and went right through the stops. I came down towards the Romney Marsh and saw it was a choice between landing in a barn or in the canal. I could not see myself landing in a barn, although I remembered having seen it done in the old Hollywood movies, so I chose the canal. The landing bent back the wings and knocked me out. When I came to, some British soldiers out on manoeuvres nearby were on the scene, and I remember one of them asking me, 'I say old chap, do you feel like a cup of tea?'

Left: On June 28, 1943, Lucas made the maiden flight in the Centaurus radial-engined Tempest II, a development of the line which was to lead into the Sea Fury. Tempest IIs were too late to see service in Europe during World War II, and plans to send a Wing to the Far East were dropped when Japan's resistance collapsed after the dropping of atomic bombs on Hiroshima and Nagasaki.

Below left: Elementary flight-test instrumentation. The first prototype Tempest II, flying from Langley, has an oversize strut thermometer attached to its port wing in between the cannon feed blisters. This was readable from the cockpit and gave the pilot an indication of air temperature when recording performance levels.

1   CARBURETTOR DUCT HEAD
2   FILTERED AIR INTAKE
3   FIREWALL (FRONT)
4   ARMOUR PLATE (FRONT)
5   MAIN FUEL TANK
6   FIREWALL (REAR)
7   OIL TANK
8   INSTRUMENT PANEL
9   JETTISONABLE SIDE PANEL (STBD)

22 ELEVATOR TRIMMING TAB
23 DOORS OVER RETRACTING TAIL WHEEL
24 LANDING WHEEL
25 INTER-SPAR FUEL TANK
26 MAGAZINE ACCESS DOORS
27 20 M/M GUNS
28 MAGAZINES
29 RETRACTABLE LANDING LAMP
30 AILERON TRIMMING TAB

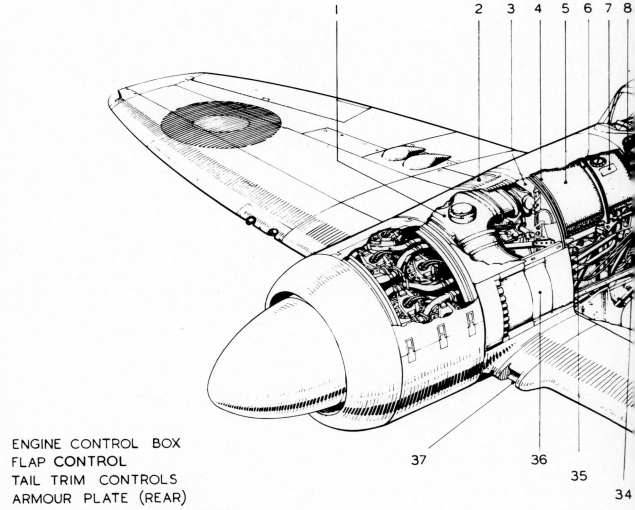

10 ENGINE CONTROL BOX
11 FLAP CONTROL
12 TAIL TRIM CONTROLS
13 ARMOUR PLATE (REAR)
14 JETTISONABLE SLIDING HOOD
15 EMERGENCY HYDRAULIC HAND PUMP
16 RADIO TRANSMITTER
17 I.F.F. INSTALLATION
18 WHIP AERIAL
19 MONOCOQUE REAR FUSELAGE
20 RUDDER TRIMMING TAB
21 TAIL NAVIGATION LAMP (PORT)

31 PRESSURE HEAD
32 FRONT GUN MOUNTINGS
33 NOSE FUEL TANK (PORT ONLY)
34 HYDRAULIC SYSTEM RESERVOIR
35 TANK FOR DE-ICING FLUID
36 ENGINE COOLING SHUTTERS
37 AIR INTAKE ENTRIES (PORT & STBD)

PREPARED BY HAWKER AIRCRAFT LIMITED

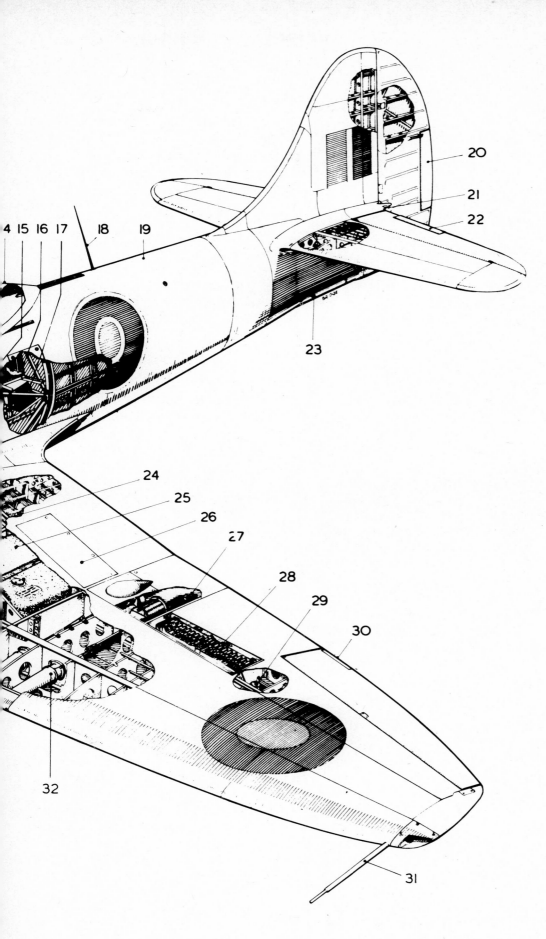

Hawkers prepared this simple, but precise cutaway drawing of the Tempest II for their repair manual which was sent with the aircraft to all squadrons.

20

21

22

23

4 15 16 17 18 19

24

25

26

27

28

29

30

32

31

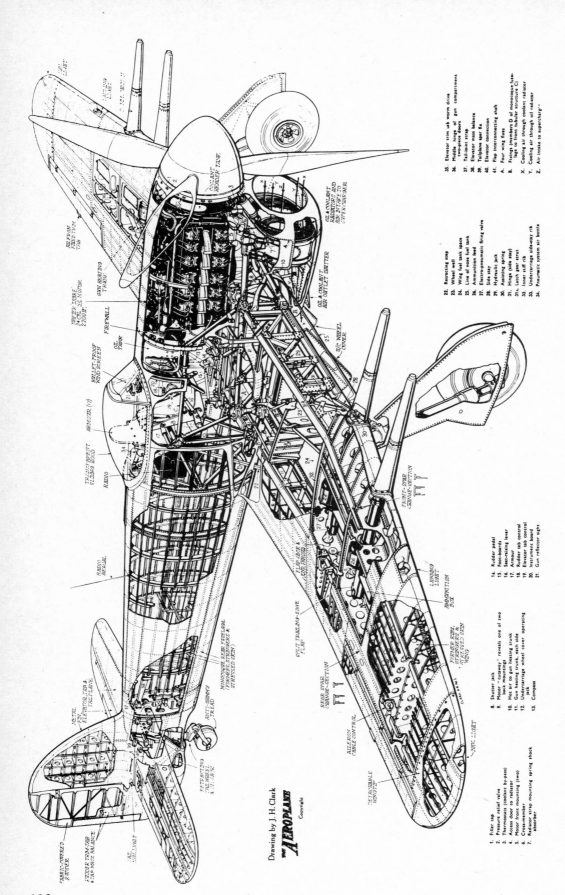

Drawing by J. H. Clark

The **AEROPLANE** Copyright

1. Filler cap
2. Pressure relief valve
3. Thermostat (coolant by-pass)
4. Access door to radiator
5. Motor front mounting
6. Cross-member
7. Radiator strap mounting shock absorber
8. Shutter jack
9. Motor "cutaway" reveals one of two back mountings
10. Hot air to gun heating trunk
11. Gun heating trunk, each side
12. Undercarriage wheel cover operating jack
13. Compass
14. Rudder pedal
15. Foot-boards
16. Seat-raising lever
17. Armour
18. Rudder tab control
19. Elevator tab control
20. Instrument board
21. Gun reflector sight.
22. Retracting step
23. Wheel well
24. Wing fuel tank space
25. Line of nose fuel tank
26. Ammunition feed
27. Electro-pneumatic firing valve
28. Side stay
29. Hydraulic jack
30. Assisting spring
31. Hinge (side stay)
31a. Latch gear strut
32. Inner stiff rib
33. Undercarriage side-stay rib
34. Pneumatic system air bottle
35. Elevator trim tab worm drive
36. Middle hinge of gun compartment
37. Two-piece doors
38. Tail-joint strap
39. Elevator mass balance
40. Tailplane spar fin
41. Elevator interconnecting shaft
42. Flap interconnecting shaft
43. Four wing fixes
8. Fixings (members D of monocoque fuselage to front tubular structure C)
X. Cooling air through coolant radiator
Y. Cooling air through oil radiator
Z. Air intake to supercharger.

Two cutaway drawings which demonstrate the differences which Camm and his design team introduced between the Typhoon (above and the Tempest V (below). The obvious main divergences from the original Typhoon layout were the thinner wing, the different shape to the tail fin with a dorsal inset, a longer nose to accommodate the fuel tank which the thin wing could not take, and a four-bladed propeller. Also, the cannons had been recessed into the wings instead of protruding menacingly as on the Typhoon.

110

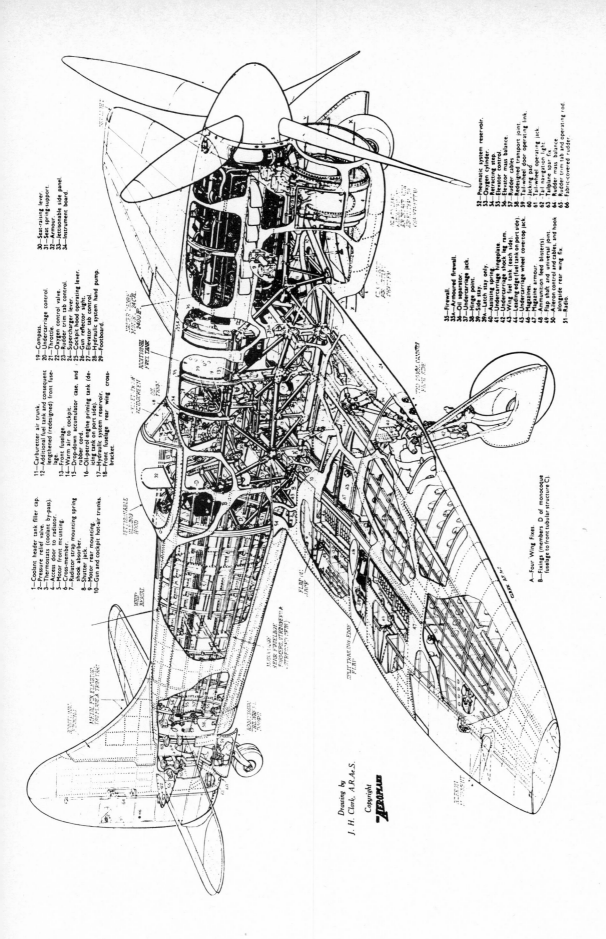

Drawing by
J. H. Clark, A.R.Ae.S.
Copyright AEROPLANE

1—Coolant header tank filler cap.
2—Pressure relief valve.
3—Thermostats (coolant by-pass).
4—Access door to radiator.
5—Motor front mounting.
6—Cross-member.
7—Radiator strap mounting spring shock absorber.
8—Shutter jack.
9—Motor rear mounting.
10—Gun and cockpit hot-air trunks.

11—Carburetter air trunk.
12—Additional fuel tank and consequent lengthened (redesigned) front fuselage.
13—Front fuselage.
14—Warm air to cockpit.
15—Drop-down accumulator case, and rubber cord.
16—Oil-petrol engine priming tank (de-icing tank on port side).
17—Hydraulic system reservoir.
18—Front fuselage rear wing cross-bracket.

19—Compass.
20—Undercarriage control.
21—Throttle.
22—Oxygen control valve.
23—Rudder trim tab control.
24—Supercharger lever.
25—Cockpit hood operating lever.
26—Gun reflector sight.
27—Elevator tab control.
28—Hydraulic system hand pump.
29—Footboard.

30—Seat-raising lever.
31—Seat spring-support.
32—Armour.
33—Jettisonable side panel.
34—Instrument board.

35—Firewall.
35A—Armoured firewall.
36—Oil separator.
37—Undercarriage jack.
38—Hinge point.
39—Side stay.
39A—Latch stay only.
40—Assisting spring.
41—Undercarriage hingeplate.
42—Undercarriage shock leg ram.
43—Wing fuel tank (each side).
43A—Leading edge (fuel tank on port side).
44—Undercarriage wheel covertop jack.
45—Magazines.
46—Magazine armour.
47—Ammunition feed blisters).
48—Ammunition feed blisters).
49—Flap shaft and universal joint.
50—Aileron control and cables, and hook alongside rear wing fix.
51—Radio.

52—Pneumatic system reservoir.
53—Oxygen cylinder.
54—Retracting step.
55—Elevator control.
56—Elevator mass balance.
57—Rudder cables.
58—Redesigned transport joint.
59—Tail-wheel door operating link.
60—Jacking pad.
61—Tail-wheel operating jack.
62—Tail navigation light.
63—Tailplane spar fix.
64—Rudder mass balance.
65—Rudder trim tab and operating rod.
66—Fabric-covered rudder.

A—Four Wing Fixes.
B—Fixings (members D of monocoque fuselage to front tubular structure C).

111

Right: Cockpit intracacies of the Tempest.

Key

1 Airspeed indicator
2 Artificial horizon
3 Rate of climb indicator
4 Altimeter
5 Direction indicator
6 Turn and bank indicator
7 Flap lever
8 Hydraulic hand pump
9 Radiator shutter lever
10 Gunsight control weapons selector box (A/C armed with bombs or rockets)
11 Undercarriage lever
12 Supercharger lever
13 Throttle friction knob
14 Throttle lever
15 Canopy winding handle
16 Reading lamp switch
17 Undercarriage emergency release switch
18 Undercarriage indicator lights
19 Beam approach button
20 Magneto switches
21 Cut-out safety control
22 Propeller pitch lever
23 Punkah louvres (late A/C only)
24 Watch holder
25 Wheel brake pressure indicators
26 T.R. 1143 control unit
27 Undercarriage indicators
28 Oxygen delivery indicator
29 Oxygen supply indicator
30 Contactor switch
31 Engine starting, boost coil switch
32 Engine starting starter switch
33 Remote contactor
34 Flap position indicator
35 Reflector sight switch
36 Cockpit light switch (port)
37 Armoured windscreen
38 Gunsight (Type Mk 1, reflected from windscreen
39 Spare bulbs for gunsight
40 Cockpit light switch (starboard)
41 Compass light switch
42 Rev counter
43 Compass card
44 Oil pressure indicator
45 Fuel pressure indicator light
46 Hood jettison lever
47 Power failure warning light
48 Boost gauge
49 Fuel contents (main tank)
50 Oil temperature indicator
51 Fuel contents (wing tanks)
52 Radiator temperature indicator
53 Punkah louvre (early A/C)
54 Cockpit heating lever
55 Verey pistol opening
56 Fuel tank pressure lever
57 Fuel cocks (inter, main, and nose tanks)

58 Cylinder priming pump
59 Engine data card
60 Signalling switch box
61 Windscreen anti-icing pumps
62 Carburettor priming pump
63 Verey pistol cartridge stowage
64 Pressure head heating switch
65 T.R. 1143 master switch
66 Heated clothing switch
67 Dimmer switch
68 Voltmeter
69 Navigation light switch
70 Resin switch
71 Camera master switch
72 Lower seat armour plate (upper armour omitted for clarity)
73 Cartridge starter reload handle
74 Gun button
75 Control column
76 Radio button
77 Push rods for aileron control
78 Elevator control push rod

79 Basic front fuselage structure of tublar steel
80 Universal joint, aileron torque tube
81 Handwheel for rudder bar adjustment
82 Compass
83 Rudder Bar
84 Heel boards (no floor as such to cockpit)
85 Elevator trim wheel
86 Rudder trim wheel

Humble in a Tempest V on test out of Langley. The aircraft is the first production model of this variation lacking the yellow 'P' for prototype on the fuselage. The picture was taken in the autumn of 1943.

Two versions of underwing, long-range tanks, indicating the development of the Typhoon-Tempest series as deep-penetration marauders into occupied Europe. (Right) On the earlier Typhoon the tank is a heavy-looking piece of equipment, but on the Tempest V (Far right) it has become streamlined and has a thinner, shorter mounting. With the latter tank, the Tempests were able to give long-range fighter cover to heavy bomber raids into Germany in the autumn of 1944.

Above right: How close can you get? A magnificent close-up of the Hawkers development pilot Bill

Right: 'Shot' from the rear cockpit of Hawkers' prototype Hart biplane registration G – ABMR, a production Tempest V from Langley, with Bill Humble at the controls, shows its aerobatic abilities. The Hart, now restored to Service colours, is in the RAF Museum, Hendon.

Far right: An unusual planform view of a Tempest V on test from Hawkers showing how the wing, on development from the Typhoon, took on the resemblance of the Spitfire. This shape was urged by the Air Ministry in view of the immense success which the Spitfire design had enjoyed during the Battle of Britain.

Below right: Perhaps the classic and best-known in-flight picture of a Tempest. With Humble at the controls, a production aircraft on test from the Hawker airfield at Langley soars gracefully above the clouds during 1944.

Far middle right: Undoubtedly the ugliest-looking aircraft of the whole series was the experimental Tempest V with an annular radiator and a ducted spinner added. The version was not proceeded with.

Far bottom right: Prototype Mark VI Tempest, in February, 1945. This version had been first flown by Bill Humble on May 9, 1944, and was fitted with a Sabre V, rated at 2,340 hp. It was planned that Tempest VIs would go into action with the RAF but the end of the war came before they could see active service. Only 142 were actually ordered, but they served in Germany and the Middle East.

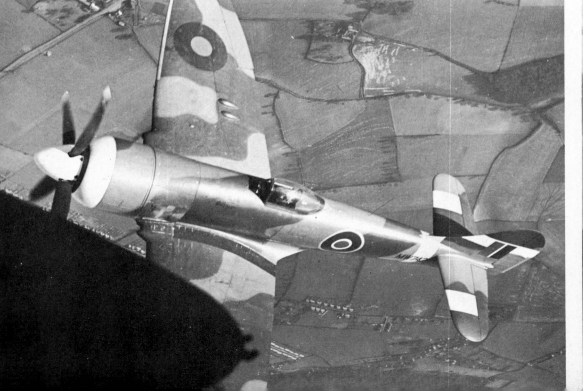

Above left: On test from Langley during 1947, a Tempest II with bomb mountings under its wings flies across the half-completed site of London airport, Heathrow.

Far left: This is the moment when the air-to-air photographer wishes that he had taken up some less hazardous profession – a Tempest II on test out of Langley eases up uncomfortably close to the tail of the camera aircraft during an aerial photo-call around the turn of the year 1944-45.

Left: At the end of a day's test flying, a production Tempest V returns to Langley and is parked against a highly-photogenic background of the setting sun. In the background is a Typhoon also on test.

Above: The first prototype Tempest was flown on September 2, 1942, by Philip Lucas, and production models (top in this picture) had a dorsal fin added to the tail. In the foreground is an experimental prototype Tempest with an annular radiator fitted experimentally to its in-line Sabre II engine in an effort to streamline the aircraft by doing away with the big scoop radiator. It was not put into production.

Building the Tempest

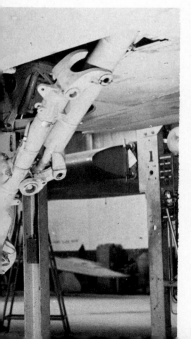

Scenes at the Hawker Langley factory during the latter stages of the war as Tempest production was well under way. (Far top left) Women aircraft workers put the finishing touches to Sabre engines, delivered from Napiers, in preparation for installation in the airframes. (Far middle left) The propeller store, with Sabres lined up, and the fin of a Tempest (top left in the picture) in the background, while in the foreground are three radial Centaurus engines, two already attached to Tempest II airframes. (Far bottom left) Tempests moving down the production line, those towards the top left with engines already fitted, those nearest the camera still waiting. In the background is another line with the aircraft in an advanced state of completion, propellers fitted. (Top left) A view straight up the production line. The aircraft nearest the camera still has to have its two halves mated, but the remainder are nearing completion. (Middle left) Sitting on a trolley to facilitate moving it about the works, a Tempest is almost complete with its engine and wings installed, but awaiting its propeller. (Bottom left) An aircraft worker operates the test rig to make sure that the under-carriage of a Tempest retracts smoothly. (Above) The fuel tank in front of the cockpit is easily visible around 40 Tempest airframes in temporary store at Langley in 1944 awaiting a supply of wings due to a strike by Hawkers workers for more pay after they had come off intensive Hurricane assembly to build up Tempest production. Because of the dispute, the RAF had only two instead of three Tempest squadrons by D-day.

Tempest Air Combat

The first fight between Tempests and enemy aircraft took place on June 8, 1944, two days after the D-Day landings, and involved two squadrons of the Newchurch Wing.

Prior to this, for some weeks leading up to the invasion, the Wing had been active in strikes against transport and airfield targets and had achieved considerable success without loss; this had contributed to a rapid increase in confidence in the new equipment and to a considerable rise in morale and aggressive spirit. The squadrons really wanted to get at the Messerschmitts and Focke-Wulfs, and on June 8 they did.

150 Wing was on air superiority patrol from Le Havre to south of the beachead

at Caen and round to Cherbourg. As Wing Leader, I was leading No 3 Squadron and No 486 (NZ) Squadron was stepped up down-sun to starboard. The twenty-four Tempests climbed south-west from Dungeness in clear morning sunlight, with only a scattered layer of fairweather cumulus clouds below at about 8,000 feet and nothing above. There was little chatter on the radio, and it was as difficult as ever to relate the beauty of this summer sky over the Channel to the serious purpose of the sortie.

The French coast soon took shape, from the Somme to port down to the Seine bay to starboard, and I increased to maximum cruise power to cross west of

A break in the storm; Tempest Vs being serviced in a pastoral setting at Newchurch soon after the invasion in June, 1944, while other members of the ground crew take their ease in front of their tents. The aircraft in the picture have the Allied invasion identification stripes over the wings and round the fuselage.

Dieppe in a shallow dive from 15,000 feet, to maintain a tactical speed of about 400mph and so reduce the chances of hits by 88mm flak in the coastal defence belt.

A brief look down on Dieppe to the left, where I had spent an uncomfortable month in hospital in 1940, and then ahead the great bends of the winding Seine showed where our turning point, Rouen, had appeared as a dark sprawl against the green and yellow landscape of rural northern France.

Suddenly Blackgang radar warned 'unidentified activity ahead, fifteen miles'.

With gunsights switched on, straps re-tightened and all eyes straining ahead

the Wing was ready; but I called to remind them to keep a sharp look out above and behind as well.

Then Blackgang again: 'Probable Bandits, 10 miles, 11 o'clock same height or below, heading your way—not positively identified'.

I levelled slightly to avoid losing height advantage and at the next call Blackgang said 'unidentifieds close ahead to port, probably a small formation and below you'.

With considerable discipline there was no word from the Tempest pilots as we strained to see something against the mottled background below of farmland, the winding Seine and the built-up areas of Rouen, with here and there small cotton-wool puffs of cloud.

And then they were there, a straggling line of single-seat fighters about 5,000 feet below, crossing from left to right ahead of us, and momentarily silhoutted against cloud.

I called, 'Aircraft 11 o'clock below, Crooner Leader going down to identify, Harlequin squadron stay up and cover'.

At about 450mph we were closing fast and when I saw the wing planform of one of them in silhouette at about two miles range for a fraction of a second I thought, 'Damn, they're Mustangs,' and I warned the others to hold their fire. But then they apparently saw us and broke violently to port with a lot of weaving and general thrashing about, I recognised them as Me 109Gs and saw black crosses at the same instant.

'Crooner Leader Tally ho! they're 109s, come on in Crooner Squadron, Harlequin Leader cover us.'

The 109 formation of about eight or nine aircraft was now pulling into a tight port turn, streaming emergency boost smoke trials, but I had to throttle back sharply to reduce our closing speed, and then in a steeply banked port turn I opened fire on the tail-ender.

At this stage there were still two other 109s in sight in front of my target, and they were all pulling white streaks of wingtip vortices as they tried to turn inside us. But our Tempests had speed and manouevre advantage, and after missing with my first burst, within one

full 360° turn I had closed to about 200yds behind and below him, and saw the second burst striking his fuselage and wing roots. This resulted in immediate violent weaving, and then the 109 pitched into a dive, with smoke billowing and almost obscuring my vision of him as I fired a third burst.

This was enough and in a steepening dive I pulled out on to his wingtip, from where I could see that the 109 was well on fire, but the pilot was not visible.

At that moment I paid the obvious penalty for not keeping a lookout behind, and the Tempest shuddered as there was a loud metallic explosion followed by a smell of cordite. I saw that a ragged hole had appeared in my starboard wing.

This was embarrassing, and pulling up in a tight spiral climb I peered back through the never-more-appreciated 'clear-view canopy' to see who was under my tail; but whoever it had been was no longer there.

Some confused radio chatter indicated that the fight was still going on somewhere, but I could see nothing except two columns of smoke hanging in the air some miles behind, and my No 2 was certainly no longer with me. So, taking what cover there was among the broken clouds, I took stock of the situation.

The hole on the wing had not seriously affected control, but it could have damaged the fuel and hydraulic systems; so I decided to see if we could get back across the Channel and sort out any landing problems when the time came.

I called Johnny Iremonger, leading 486 Squadron, to rendezvous the Wing over Rouen and continue the patrol at his discretion since 486 had not been engaged; and I confirmed that I was returning to base damaged and unaccompanied. Someone called from 3 Squadron to confirm my 'flamer', and I told him, 'Thanks, but shut up'!

One of 486 Squadron aircraft called in to say he had propeller trouble and would bale out, but as we were quite close to the beachhead area I told him to try for the emergency landing ground which our briefing had indicated would be opened on this day. This he did and landed safely, though under fire from enemy ground forces. He was returned to us by the Navy next day.

Meantime, my Tempest was still flying, though slowly, and the fuel gauges gave normal indications. So I headed back north for the French Channel coast, hoping that there were no more 109s about. After a very long thirty minutes I saw the hazy outline of the south coast ahead.

Crossing in over Hastings, I confirmed to control that I intended to return to Newchurch. Although it was pleasant to see the tents and dispersals of the airfield still bathed in sunshine, there remained the small matter of whether the undercarriage was damaged and if a safe landing could be made.

Telling Flying Control the problem, I brought the Tempest in low over them

for a visual check, and they reported a large hole on the underside of the wing as well, which was not encouraging.

However, with speed reduced to 110mph, I selected 'undercarriage down', and it locked with comforting green lights. I still did not know if the brakes were unaffected, although the differential pressures looked good. A gentle landing executed with more than usual care gave no trouble, and then we were bouncing across the rough field to the 3 Squadron dispersal.

A lot had happened in the past hour and a half and I could not immediately appreciate my good fortune out of concern for the state of my Tempest 'RB', and until the Wing was safely back. But a quick look underneath with the ground crew confirmed that the damage was confined to holes top and bottom of the wing and the starboard under-

carriage leg fairing which had completely blown away. RB was repairable, and then Johnny Iremonger came in sight leading the Wing low overhead in reasonable, if slightly excited formation, and I could see that we had lost no-one else.

Whether the 109 leader had got round at me for a wide angle deflection shot while I was busy with the tail-ender, or whether I had intercepted some of the shot and shell pouring forth from the Tempests behind me we never discovered; but the Tempests had started their score with four 109s destoyed and two others damaged, and we were all satisfied — all that is except the 486 New Zealanders who reckoned that their Pommie Wing Leader had kept them up as top cover to keep them out of the way!

RPB

Ranging far and wide over the enemy – occupied Channel coast before D-Day, the first Tempests to go into squadron service helped to soften-up the area ready for the invasion. These camera gun pictures, all taken on one day by Beamont's aircraft from Newchurch, show hits on goods trains in the coastal belt.

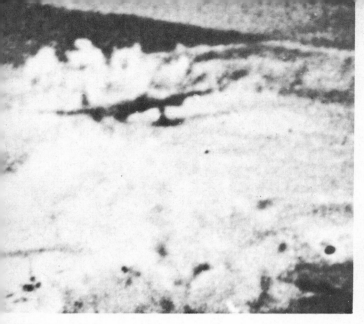

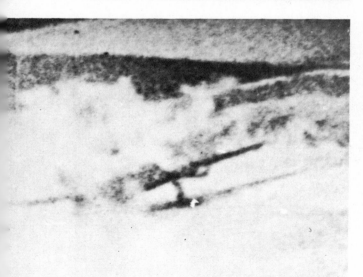

A tip from Intelligence that the German bomber force on Pontoise airfield, just north of Paris, had been reinforced by the arrival of a squadron of ten Junkers Ju 188 bombers sent a flight of six Tempest Vs of 3 Squadron on a sortie in late May, 1944. They arrived over the enemy base at 6 pm catching the 188s as they were on the ground being prepared for an attack on Bristol that night. The three camera-gun pictures from Beamont's aircraft shows the havoc wreaked by the Tempests, whose pilots later claimed five of the ten bombers. This operation gave the Tempests their first major success. A reconnaissance picture of Pontoise taken the following day. Some of the destroyed 188s are marked with crosses.

The Malignant Robots

In spite of industrial strikes, technical troubles, and the icy grasp of officialdom, the Tempest proved to be the right aircraft in the right place at the right time when the first of Hitler's 'revenge' weapons, the V-1 'doodlebugs', started to rain on London in the middle of June, 1944. The fight against these 'malignant robots', as they were aptly called by one high-ranking RAF officer, proved to be one of the most significant chapters in the brief wartime story of the Tempest. Thanks to its superior performance, 632 V-1s failed to reach their primary target — a third of all those shot down by the RAF, and roughly one-sixth of all those destroyed.

The first whisper of the forthcoming onslaught by the Germans' pilotless flying bombs came to Beamont in March, 1944, when he was summoned to see the Air Office Commanding II Group, Sir Hugh Saunders, and asked to form the first Tempest wing. Saunders gave him a privileged glimpse of a map of the Channel showing the areas where the invasion was to be, and told him that the wing should be located within the shortest possible reaction time from the Pas de Calais. From a list of four airfields, Beamont chose Newchurch, near Dungeness, in Kent. Saunders' comment was, 'I'm glad you've chosen that one, because you are in the right area for the V-weapons. Do you know anything about them?' Beamont was told that the government expected that one of them would be the V-1, followed later by high-altitude, high-velocity rockets, against which there was no known defence — although the Tempests would be expected to act on intelligence information and attack their launching sites.

'That', Beamont commented after the meeting, 'sounds like a fairly busy summer.' And a busy summer it did turn out to be for the Tempests. Aircraft from the wing were first scrambled against V-1s at 5.30am in the morning of June 16. By the night of the same day, their score was already eight. Not that bringing down the doodlebugs was easy. Propelled by a pulse-jet engine mounted on top of the fuselage at the rear, the doodlebugs sped through the skies of south-east England at between 340 and 370mph. Their wing span was only 16 feet and their length 20 feet, making them a minute target for the fighter pilots against the landscape background at the height of 1,500-2,500 feet at which the V-1s normally flew. According to the description of one of the fighter pilots engaged in combating them, they were bronze on top and pale blue underneath, with the 'stove pipe' engine exhaust glowing white hot. Each carried one ton of high explosive, and were crudely manufactured by the Germans at a cost of around £120 each.

Coming up on them from astern, the Tempest pilots found they had a target only three feet wide across the fuselage, and with wings only eight inches thick to aim at. Despite the fact that they scored early successes, the defenders found themselves missing frequently as they learned the new game. Firing from 400 yards was too wasteful, but if the Tempests went close in, to 200 yards, the resultant explosion of one ton of HE was likely to blow up the pursuer as well as the pursued. Pilots returned to base with the fabric burned off the rudders of their aircraft, and with their arms scorched where flames from disintegrating V-1s had seared through the cockpit air vents.

Buck Feldman tells exactly how it was: 'In the Newchurch wing, we heard the first V-1s come across. The gunners opened up over 180 degrees and the shrapnel was falling all over the airfield and going through our tents. One P-47 Thunderbolt fired at a V-1 over the airfield and the bullet drilling a hole through the hand of one of our airmen lying asleep in his bed. After we had first been scrambled on June 16, we had finished our patrol and were going back to Newchurch when we heard on the radio that there was a V-1 crossing near Ashford. The sky was overcast, but there was a big ray of sunshine coming through a hole in the clouds.

'The V-1 broke out in front of me. I was right underneath it, and let fly for two or three seconds. When I was only 50 yards away, it blew up in my face. My wing man saw me disappear in a sheet of

Air Commodore C. A. Bouchier, as senior air staff officer of II Group in 1944, was in overall charge of Tempest operations against flying bombs. He co-operated closely with Beamont on the day-to-day tactics, and authorised the plan which excluded most other Allied fighters from chasing V1s over a wide area of south east England after Tempest pilots had been baulked by slower aircraft.

flame and shouted, 'You are on fire. Bale out.' I thought I had had it, and I found later that the aeroplane in places was burned and blackened.'

The problem of concentrating gunfire on these tiny, fast-moving targets was solved through a piece of unofficial action by Beamont. Seeing that the standard Fighter Command 'spread harmonization' pattern for the guns was unsuitable for operation against flying bombs, he asked for official permission to point-harmonize his own guns at 300 yards. This was not forthcoming, but Beamont went ahead anyway. On the next sortie he found he was able to hit the V-1s with his opening burst, and he then ordered all 150 Wing guns to be similarly treated. As he later wrote, 'This had two results; the first was an immediate and sustained improvement in the Wing's scoring rate, and the second was a different sort of rocket from headquarters!'

Finding and then hitting their robot adversaries was not the only problem which was encountered by the Tempest pilots. They also had to contend with the enthusiasm for the chase and the kill among their RAF and United States Army Air Force comrades in the air, and with that of the army anti-aircraft gunners on the ground. Within a few days of the attack beginning, the sky over south-east England was a whirlpool of Allied fighters desperately manoeuvring around each other to get in a shot at the invaders, and trying to dodge, as they did so, the shell-bursts of their own side's ack-ack. It was all largely uncoordinated, and it was seriously reducing the effectiveness of the pilots of the Tempests which, apart from a few Spitfire XIIs and XIVs, and Mustangs with uprated engines, were the only aircraft with sufficient speed to overhaul the V-1s.

There were some casualties from friendly fire during this period. In the first week of the battle, two Tempest pilots were shot down by anti-aircraft guns. This story soon gained currency among the local population, with the result that deputations were sent to the local MPs, and questions were asked in the House. The Tempest Wing had their own more immediate satisfaction, however, when by complete coincidence one of them downed a V-1 into the grounds of a country house used as a mess by the gunners. The resulting explosion blew out all the windows in the mess without hurting anybody, just as the gunner officers were having their breakfast. The Tempest pilots were said to have come back from that particular sortie holding their sides.

To sort out the defensive tangle, Beamont went to 11 Group headquarters and asked for a special defence zone to be established in the area bounded by Folkestone, Eastbourne, Guildford and Croydon, in which all aircraft would be banned except those few squadrons which were fast enough to deal with the V-1s. Beamont also suggested that the Royal Observer Corps should deploy round the coast with signal rockets which

they would fire towards any V-1 which they spotted approaching, so helping the radar-vectored fighters to identify their small, fast-moving prey. Both suggestions were immediately accepted by Air Vice-Marshal Bouchier, and the Tempests and the other fast fighters began at once to achieve further improvement in their kill rate.

All through this period, the Tempests of 150 Wing — 32 at the beginning, rising to 48 at the end — were being operated with their engines flat out, a factor which resulted in wear and tear problems later in the year when the squadrons went into Europe to operate. In addition to their daytime activities, the Wing also put up half a dozen interception patrols each night between 11.30pm and 3am, as there was no pause in the bombardment, the Germans firing off their flying bombs at any hour of the 24, just as soon as they were ready.

At one stage of the battle, in fact, as many V-1s were coming across during the short summer hours of darkness as during the day. Towards the end, RAE Farnborough perfected a simple optical gunsight for use at night, in which the pilot saw two images of the target flame until they came together at firing range. This was fitted to a special squadron of night-fighting Tempests which was based at Manston, Kent, and also to some Mosquito squadrons which took part in the battle — and was very effective.

Initially, the 150 Wing Tempests proceeded on a trial and error basis at night, feeling their way, without any previous experience of intercepting and attacking a brilliant light — which was all that could be seen of the V-1. Beamont described an experimental sortie from Newchurch as follows: 'The radar interception was made far easier than in daytime by virtue of the fact that the brilliant flame of the pulse-jet could be seen at night for ten or 15 miles in good weather, and all one had to do was to close at full throttle until at firing range.

'But here was the problem. With nothing by which to judge distance, except a light which got progressively bigger and more dazzling, it was not easy to get into an effective firing range without suddenly overshooting and possibly even running into the target. I found that the best method was to approach the target from astern until we appeared to be within about 1,000 yards, and then to descend below it until in a relative position of approximately 100 feet below and 300 yards behind.

'This could be judged reasonably well by looking up through the transparent canopy and over the top of the windscreen arch. From this situation, a gentle climb was made into the dead-astern position until, preferably, the wake of the V-1 was felt in the Tempest. Then, with the gunsight centred directly on the exhaust flame, a long burst was generally enough to deal with it.'

As the weeks went by the Newchurch Tempests were under increasing pressure, with activity against the V-1s around the clock. A consolation was that as they became more knowledgeable about their adversary they became more skilful, and their scores rose. The pilots became some of the sharpest shots in the RAF. And if, for some reason, the guns failed, or ammunition ran out, the 'malignant robots' could be downed by other methods. The V-1s were gyro-controlled, and the Tempest pilots found that it was possible to fly across the front of them and knock them off course and over with their slipstream. Also, by flying alongside and raising a wingtip under one of those flying of the flying bomb, the boundary layer of air around the wing would be disturbed, and they would topple.

By the middle of August, the battle against the flying bombs was virtually over as far as the Tempests were concerned, as the anti-aircraft guns, so wild in the early days of the battle, gained the measure of their targets. This was due to the introduction of greatly-improved radar-aiming predictors, and shells with fuses designed to explode in proximity to the targets. Tempest pilots considered the new-found expertise of the gunners highly frustrating. Buck Feldman: "I shot down 11 V-1s in all, and had eight further interceptions, but the guns got there first each time.

'Two of my kills were at night. Control had a system of searchlights on the coast between Hastings and Dungeness, with two shining out to sea and two shining upwards. This was the point around which the Tempests were stacked, flying figures of eight, waiting for the V-1s to come over. When the bottom aircraft left the stack, the others would move down. It was an unpopular operation, as it was necessary to fly with navigation lights on to avoid mid-air collisions, and the Germans tried to infiltrate their own aircraft into the pattern. Control would broadcast the code phrase, 'Close your windows' when there was an intruder, as a signal to switch off our navigation lights.'

Although the Germans continued to send V-1s over for the rest of 1944 — the last one fell on British soil as late as March 29, 1945 — the menace was virtually mastered by the end of August. The final tally was awesome — 6,700 bombs despatched, almost 4,000 of which were brought down by fighters, the guns, or barrage balloons. Those which did get through killed 5,500 people, injured a further 16,000, destroyed 23,000 houses, and caused damage to 750,000. At the height of the onslaught, on August 2, 316 V-1s were launched at the capital, of which 100 penetrated. The average throughout the worst period sent against Britain was 100 a day, but so successful did the defenders become that by the end of August, of 97 despatched in one 24-hour period, only four reached their target.

The part played by Tempests in this part of the defence of Great Britain was crucial, and has never been fully acknowledged so far. A total of fewer than 30 aircraft was available initially, building up to 114 by September, and these knocked out 632 V-1s. Had the Tempests not been ready and in position in time, that figure might well have dwindled to 200, and the situation among the civilian population could have become catastrophic, with a further 400 or more doodlebugs falling on London instead of upon the farmlands of Kent, Sussex and Surrey, or exploding harmlessly in the air.

Above: King George VI presents a DFC to Buck Feldman, an American serving with a Tempest squadron in July, 1944, in an informal airfield ceremony at Blackbushe.

Right: A graphic illustration in a booklet produced at the end of the war by the south London borough of Croydon showing how the area was peppered by V-1 doodlebugs during the summer of 1944, killing 211 people, and injuring almost 2,000 others. If the Tempests had not stood between congested areas such as this and the onslaught of the malignant robots, the toll of the civilian population of the capital and their homes would have been far worse.

Far top right: Tempests were among the few RAF fighters with sufficient speed to overhaul the V-1s when they began arriving in the summer of 1944, and their success is graphically reflected by the poster for the 'Doodlebug Celebration Dance' on July 20 that year to celebrate 150 Wing's marksmanship.

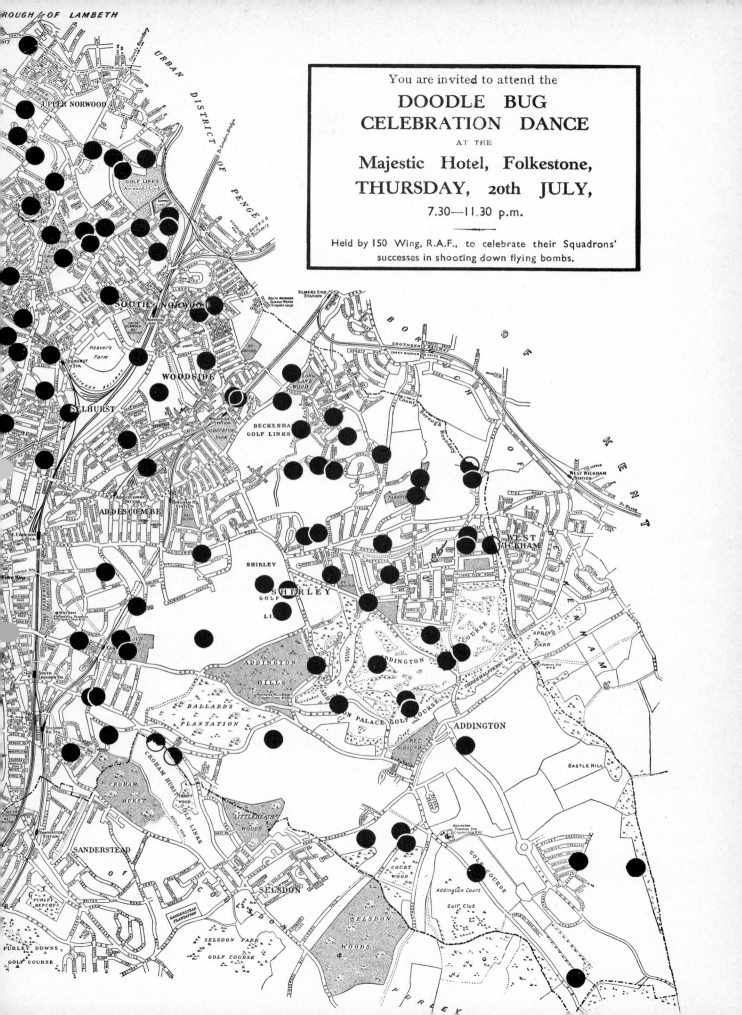

You are invited to attend the

DOODLE BUG
CELEBRATION DANCE

AT THE

Majestic Hotel, Folkestone,
THURSDAY, 20th JULY,

7.30—11.30 p.m.

Held by 150 Wing, R.A.F., to celebrate their Squadrons'
successes in shooting down flying bombs.

FLYING BOMB ON LAUNCHING PLATFORM

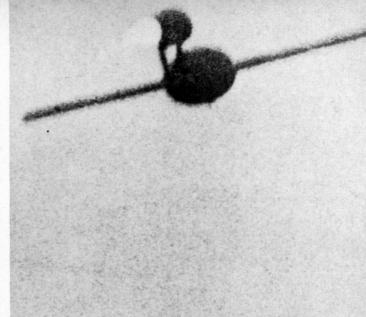

Above left: This RAF photo-reconnaissance picture taken over northern France in June, 1944, shows a V-1 flying bomb ready for launching on its ramp, pointing towards its target – London. Such sites were difficult to spot and were heavily defended.

Left: A remarkable shot taken from a second aircraft of a Tempest V of 150 Wing over Kent in the summer of 1944 pursuing a V-1 flying bomb, which can be seen as a small, black cross (top right in picture). The picture illustrates clearly the low altitude at which many of these combats were fought over the fields of south east England.

Above: Tempest Vs took close-up pictures of German V-1 pilotless flying bombs as they were hunted in the skies of south-east England in the summer of 1944. The flame coming out of the rear of the pulse jets mounted on the top of the rear of the 'doodlebug' – as the bombs were colloquially known – can be clearly seen.

Although the German V-1s were pilotless, attacking them could be a dangerous affair for the Tempest pilots. They were small targets, and it was necessary to go in close to make sure of hits – at which the doodlebugs were apt to blow up, sometimes taking the attacking fighters with them. (Top right) This series of camera gun shots shows the risk which the pilots took as the target comes into range. (Middle right) His first cannon shells begin to register and smoke begins to develop (Bottom right). The V-1 explodes at only 300 yards range. (Far top right) The fireball grows as the one-ton load of high explosive, and the fuel, go up. (Far middle right) The Tempest is committed to penetrating the fireball and at this distance the pilot could feel the intense heat, and probably had his hands scorched where hot air was drawn in through the ventilators (Far bottom right) He has pulled safely away through the fire, but a new hazard is the flying pieces of the disintegrated V-1, including the stove-pipe engine exhaust, seen at an angle bottom centre.

Tempest Ground Attack

In the neglected garden of the farm cottage at Newchurch which served as Wing flying headquarters and dispersal accommodation for No 3 Fighter Squadron, the readiness pilots were sprawled out in various attitudes of heat exhaustion in the grilling summer sunshine.

The 'Ops' telephone shrilled and nearly fell off the windowsill of my office where, as Wing Leader, I had perched it within reach of my deck-chair.

Identifying myself to the 11 Group operations staff officer at the other end, I said: 'What's the form', and he replied: 'We've a target for you near Pontoise if you'd like to try it.' (This in deference to the fact that we had only very recently declared our new Tempests 'operational',

and Group were not yet sure of our capabilities.)

He went on: 'It is a suspected reinforcement of twin-engined bombers prior to a raid tonight — Johnny Johnston's wing reported seeing them'.

Though tempted, I refrained from asking what the Spitfires had done about it, knowing that they were most probably on a medium or high-altitude fighter sweep and only looking for airborne targets. I said we would be delighted.

Group said that the target areas would be the southern dispersals. I was to take one squadron and, 'yes, there was flak.' A form 'd' was on the way and, tactics were at the leaders' discretion.

Checking with the Wing intelligence section confirmed the position of half-a-dozen flak posts and an 88mm site near the town of Pontoise. As we would be arriving at about 6pm on what looked like being a perfect summer evening, I planned a run-in which would keep us clear of the heavy flak and allow an attack out of the eye of the westering sun. The No 3 Squadron Tempests fired up along their dispersal as I started RB on time, and with their CO, Alan Dredge, following behind my No 2, Bruce Cole, we taxied out over Newchurch's undulating Summerfelt track runway with grass already turning brown in the dry weather.

After a check behind at the Tempests lined up in pairs, I held up my hand and dropped it forward to signal 'take-off'; and opening up power smoothly to about 90 percent, to leave a margin for the No 2, accelerated down the rough strip with Bruce's Tempest close in to starboard.

Undercarriage up and reducing to cruise-climb power in a gentle left-hand climbing turn, to allow the others to join up initially in pairs astern, I called control, 'Harlequin aircraft setting course', and received a terse acknowledgement. There would now be radio silence except for operational necessity.

The shining Channel unfolded as we climbed out past Dungeness, and at 5,000 feet I could already see the grey outline of the enemy coast at Cap Griz Nez. On my brief wing rock to signal 'open out', the Tempests slid out on

either side into a four-pair 'search' formation, and I looked back with a never-failing sense of pleasure at these slim, purposeful fighters rising and falling gently. Their pilots, my good friends, were clear in every detail except for their masked faces, as they sat high in their clear-vision cockpit canopies. Every sortie was a challenge, as it had been since 1939. This was 1944, with the invasion imminent; what would today bring?

The radio suddenly broke into my train of thought as Alan Dredge called with a falling oil pressure and peeled away from the formation with his No 2, which was standard practice in emergency. I confirmed the action, wishing him luck, and re-checked the course to our first landmark, the Somme estuary.

Now we were down to six aircraft, which reduced our effectiveness and probably increased the risk factor as we would have fewer guns to bring to bear on the defences. But there were the sand dunes of Le Treport to port, and a hazy line ahead indicated the French coast stretching towards Dieppe in the south-west. The sky was clear; it was a perfect day for a dogfight.

Control called as we crossed in at 10,000 feet, with Abbeville over to port, and said: 'No trade', but I told the squadron to keep a sharp look-out in any case, as I would now be preoccupied with navigation. I had got to know most of the area well since 1939, but had never been to Pontoise or the Paris area before, and the next five minutes could be critical if I missed the track.

But the villages, railways and woods along the track line on my map appeared in the appropriate order and position, and suddenly there was the aerodrome of Cormeille en Vexin, with a white concrete runway and perimeters contrasting against green airfield grass.

Calling, 'Target area to port, going down in 10 secs', I pulled the harness straps tight, lowered the seat one notch for gunsight vision, switched on the sight, and made a final adjustment to brilliance on the reostat, while searching hard for our targets.

At first, from two to three miles at

10,000 feet, the airfield looked peaceful and deserted and I wondered for a moment if our effort was going to be abortive. But then I saw them — one, two, three and more dark twin-engined aircraft in a long dispersal area among woods, well south of the airfield towards a wide bend in the now-visible, winding Seine.

'OK fellows, targets on the south side. Harlequin leader taking left-hand dispersal. Spread out, echelon starboard and take individual targets. Going down NOW. Make this a good one!''

One always said this, but it was redundant as these tremendous fighter pilots could be relied upon utterly and to the death if necessary — this was what it was all about — the sure knowledge of reliance upon the others in the team. Times and values change, but these were the values of that time.

And this was where the qualities of the Tempest shone. Steady and undemanding in trimmed, cruise formation, it was instantly responsive and well damped and crisp in manoeuvre. As I rolled away into a dive to port, I knew that when the target area appeared in the windscreen I would be able to track the gunsight onto the target smoothly and with little over-correction even in turbulence.

So it was now. In anticipation of flak I had decided to attack at high speed and steadied at about 470mph passing 5,000 feet. A quick glance behind to see the Tempests lining up to starboard and following closely, and so into the attack!

My target was clearly a black-painted Ju 88 (subsequently identified as a very new 188 version) in a high-walled blast pen. A short ranging burst and then hard down on the trigger, ruddering corrections as necessary as the blast pen erupted in strikes, with bursts all over the bomber and a large piece of it flying in the air as I snatched at the stick at the last moment to avoid flying headlong into the target.

Then came the flak, sparks and streaks across the canopy, and grey puffs of smoke and dust from shells bursting on the ground ahead, and continuous flashes from a gunpost up a wooded slope to the left.

Now was the time for some really low

flying, and with full throttle and fine pitch my Tempest continued at 50 feet or less, and about 450mph across runways, past a control tower with gun or shell bursts round it, up the side of a hill and, jinking round the corner of Pontoise village.

Looking back, there were columns of smoke from our targets, shell bursts and weaving tracer everywhere, and the Tempests jinking after me.

'Keep down low', I called, 'and pull up with me at five miles'.

Then it was over, and we were climbing homewards at 5,000 feet over France in the golden evening sun, with the other Tempests, all five of them, sliding back into formation.

Even from 10,000 feet, columns of smoke from the target area were still in sight; otherwise the sky was clear and serene over northern France, and in our confined cockpits it was difficult to relate the tense excitement that we still felt to

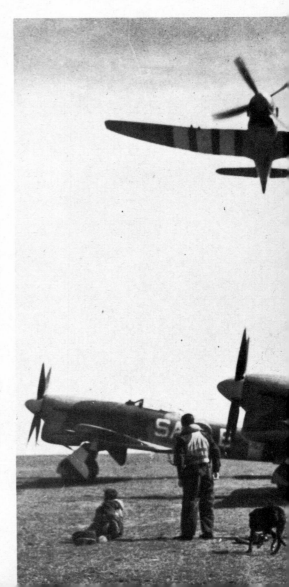

the now apparently quiet cruise back to base.

There could be no relaxing vigilance, for the 190s and 109s could well attack anywhere, and often attempted radar intercepts at easily-identified landmarks such as crossing-out points. But on this occasion there was no activity, and when control confirmed this I told them, 'Not to worry — we had a good prang!'

With the familiar green-grey vee of Dungeness jutting out towards us ahead, I called the Tempests into close formation and we swept across Newchurch, golden in the evening light in a tightly-compact group of three pairs before pulling up into a left-hand circuit in starboard echelon for a continuous-curve approach and stream landing at 200 yard intervals on the rough tracking runway.

As I led the six Tempests back to 3 Squadron dispersal, I opened the canopy and unfastened my oxygen mask to breathe the warm air, with its scent of farmland, hot hedgerows and the inevitable high-octane exhaust smoke, and I enjoyed an almost physical sense of wellbeing. We had struck a good blow at the enemy; we had probably saved some lives in a coming bombing raid; we had built up further confidence in our new Tempests, which had been magnificent, and we had lost no-one in the process.

I swung RBs tail round in the dispersal, sending a shower of dried grass into the air, and cut the engine.

One by one, the others coughed and spluttered to silence. Then the ground crew, excited by the smoke-grimed guns, swarmed onto the wing.

As the fitter helped take off my straps he asked, 'any luck, sir?', and he listened with dawning amazement as I spoke of our attack. The he said, 'We didn't think you went on operations — we thought you were only a test pilot'.'

RPB

Below left: As a Tempest pilot beats up the airfield in the spring of 1944, his colleagues on the ground by their aircraft take scarcely any notice – although the din must have been tremendous. The wing leader's aircraft is in the foreground.

Below: In a picture specially taken on April 15, 1944, at Newchurch to pulicize the new Tempest V fighters, a New Zealand pilot, Flying Officer Jimmy Cullen, poses before the massive four-bladed propeller of his aircraft.

The Drive into Europe

At the end of their participation in the flying-bomb battle, many Tempests were withdrawn from service temporarily for major work to be carried out on their engines. By that time, the aircraft was being adjudged by many as the best low/medium altitude fighter to reach squadron service during the war, and most RAF officers remained of this opinion when victory in Europe came in 1945. The Tempest had also proved itself in a series of mock battles carried out over the south of England in the summer of 1944 against American fighters flown by skilled United States Army Air Force pilots. The verdict was that, flown skilfully, it could see off the excellent P-51D Mustang, while it completely overshadowed the P-47D Thunderbolt.

Typhoons, meanwhile, played the paramount close-support role for the British Army as it advanced into Europe During the D-Day landings, early in June, 1944, they softened up the defences with their devastating rocket salvoes, and were called in by the Americans to work on the beaches after their own bombers had left bunkers intact. In the fierce battles which raged in Normandy as the Allied forces pushed inland, the Typhoons came up against the Panzers, including the giant German Tiger tanks. Cannon shells of the fighters simply bounced off the flanks of these monsters, but the rockets were able to cause crippling damage to their tracks. The Cab Rank system which had evolved in the desert campaigns, and which was perfected in Europe, had squadrons of Typhoons flying standing patrols just behind the battlefront, waiting for calls for assistance from Allied armies below.

Directed by RAF ground control liaison officers based in armoured vehicles near the front line, they were able to saturate targets within seconds of being called. Each operation needed pin-point accuracy and split-second timing, as the targets to which the Typhoons were sent were often as close as 150 yards to the Allies' own line. The targets included machine-gun posts, troops on the move and convoys, as well as gun emplacements and Panzer tanks. To avoid confusion, the enemy targets would be indicated with bursts of red smoke, the Allied positions with yellow.

Although the effect of the rocket attacks was devastating, the losses from such low-level flying in the face of heavy ground fire were also heavy. But production of Typhoons was at its peak, and aircraft were queueing up to have a crack at the targets; so a limit of five minutes was placed on each attack before another section was allowed to take over. In all, 23 squadrons equipped with Typhoons served with the 2nd Tactical Air Force in 1944/45. Nine others, with Fighter Command, augmented them from Britain.

Tempests had joined their mates from the Hawker stable fairly briefly during the D-Day operations, when all 24 aircraft of 150 Wing went on beachhead patrol. On D-Day + 2 the Tempests met enemy fighters for the first time when in a dogfight over Rouen three, and possibly four, Me 109Gs were destroyed. Even earlier than that, in May, the first operational Tempests had ranged over northern France. On the 21st of that month they destroyed a midget submarine and its transporter near Coutrai; six days later, in what was the first Tempest attack on an airfield, a group of Ju 188s being prepared at Pontoise, outside Paris, for a night raid on southern England were shot up and four were either damaged or destroyed.

Typhoons played a vital role in the run-up period to Operation Overlord — the D-Day landings — with their participation in the Channel Stop operation. In this, virtually every enemy

Tempest leaders; Beamont and 'Digger' Cotes Preedy, commanding officer of No 3 Squadron, at 122 Wing mess at Grimbergen, Brussels, in October, 1944. Until a week previously the mess had been occupied by the Luftwaffe. The object of Beamont's interest is an American cap badge, one of collection of such trophies which Cotes Preedy had assembled on his flying jacket.

ship afloat was either sunk, rendered useless, or chased into port, and the chain of radar posts on the French coast which would have warned of the Allied final approach was attacked repeatedly.

One last anxiety over the serviceability of the Typhoons came soon after the first squadrons landed on, and began to operate from, continental soil. It was soon discovered that the engines were refusing to start — a fault which was rapidly traced, through cooperation between Hawker, Napier and the Services, to the fact that the Normandy landing fields contained a high level of quartz dust an abrasive mineral which, sucked in through the big air scoop, was gradually grinding the powerplants to pieces. A modification in the form of an air filter was quickly devised and introduced in the field in a remarkable support action by Hawkers. The Typhoons were soon back in full operation once more.

Philip Lucas was involved in that 'fix', and in another, stranger case, in which a Canadian wing were threatening not to fly the Typhoon after two of their aircraft had burst into flames and crashed while attacking an apparently-undefended bridge. The theory was that the fuel vents of the aircraft had become clogged through the corrosive effects of standing out near the Normandy beaches, causing fuel to flood the gun bays and producing flashbacks when the guns were fired. But when the front line moved up shortly afterwards, a visit to the crashed machines proved that they had, in fact, been shot down. This fully satisfied the Canadians, who said that while they objected to being killed by technical faults, they were quite prepared to take their chance with the Germans.

Before they moved into Europe, after completing their defence against the V-1 flying bombs, the Tempests were sent against the V-2 rocket sites in Holland, using long-range tanks to cover the distances involved. These were difficult targets, as not only were they small and well-concealed, but they were also heavily defended. According to the pilots: 'All hell broke out' when they arrived overhead.

A second task at this time, also requiring the use of the long-range tanks, was escorting RAF Halifax and Lancaster bombers on their way to raid Germany. The rendezvous would be at 18,000 feet over the German border with Holland, some 200 miles from the Tempests' base in Britain. It was never difficult to pinpoint, as the bomber stream could be spotted from 30 miles or more away, surrounded by intense flak bursts. The Tempest squadrons would escort them as far as their fuel reserves would allow, and then turn for home, leaving the bombers to battle their way towards their targets in the Ruhr.

Tempests began to join Typhoons on what had been enemy ground in September, 1944, when Beamont's Wing flew to Grimbergen, north of Brussels to join 122 Wing. On their first day in Belgium, they engaged Fw 190s over the Rhine, destroying three. At Volkel, near Eindhoven, in Holland, Tempest squadrons shared the battered airfield with Typhoon squadrons, with the Germans still dug in just over the airfield boundary. The Tempest pilots were luckier than their comrades in being just out of range of the enemy guns. They took great delight in waiting each morning until the methodical Germans put a short barrage down on to the Typhoon pilots' area, before calling up their wing leader on the operations telephone and getting him out of the dug-out where he was taking shelter from the blitz.

As the Allied forces swept on towards the German borders during the winter of 1944-45, the Tempest established itself as one of the most successful ground attack and battlefield superiority fighters in the European theatre of operations. The main factors contributing to this were speed, controllability, weapons accuracy, and superior all-round and attack vision. Additional factors were high pilot morale, and proficiency following the unique period of gunnery opportunity against the small, fast targets presented by the flying bombs.

The Tempest proved to have a general ease of operation and a relatively low accident rate. With its wide-track undercarriage, and effective controls right down to the stall, it was less critical to land in crosswinds or turbulence than the Spitfire. On occasions when, due to defects or operational damage, landings had to be made with one main leg down and the other hung up, these were usually successful.

There were casualties among the Tempest pilots, of course, one of these being Beamont himself. According to the history of 122 Wing, published in Germany in November, 1945, he was taken prisoner-of-war after attacking with a formation of eight Tempests a packed troop train protected by flak. During the first attack, troops were seen leaping out of the windows in large numbers. On the second attack the engine at one end blew up. Beamont made a third attack with the eight aircraft, finally leaving the train smashed and blazing from end to end. Unfortunately, while re-forming the Tempests, the wing commander's machine started to stream glycol, and he had to forceland shortly afterwards. He made an excellent belly landing, and called up to say he was O.K.

The history tells of another Tempest pilot who was shot down while attacking a train a little later during the invasion period. Squadron Leader K. F. Thiele had completed two tours with Bomber Command before transferring to fighters. On February 10 he was hit by flak and 'baled out and landed in a station yard. Unfortunately, the platform was crowded with Germans waiting patiently for a train to arrive. As Jimmy Thiele had just spoilt their hopes of a punctual trip by puncturing the engine, the crowd was distinctly hostile when he floated down into its midst, and tried to push him under a passing goods train. Rescued from this predicament, he exchanged a few words with the 19-year-old flak segeant who had shot him down, and was removed to internment.'

Some indication of the number of targets of opportunity which abounded in that final run-up towards the end of the war can be gained by the fact that, during February 1944, 122 Wing accounted for the record total of 484 German locomotives, 32 aircraft, 485 road vehicles, 118 barges and 650 railway trucks. There were many examples of individual bravery, including that of Flight Lieutenant Burne, a Tempest pilot with 41 squadron, who was hit by flak and severly injured. Burne, who had previously lost a leg in Sumatra, sustained multiple fractures to his right arm and a bad wound in his chest. In spite of this, he brought his aircraft back to base. When he arrived overhead, another pilot was asking for priority in landing, so Burne went round again. For this feat, he was awarded the DSO.

The 21st Army crossed the Rhine on March 24, 1945, with the Typhoons and Tempests of 2nd TAF continuing to soften up the way in front. But as the German borders were overrun the resistance became more frantic, with the defenders throwing virtually everything that could fly into the fight. This included their very latest jet-powered fighter, Messerschmitt Me 262, which provided the Typhoons and Tempests with a real headache as it was around 100mph faster than even the latter. Buck Feldman recalls. 'They used to take up

position on our wings, and then climb away vertically when we turned to meet them. The only way we managed to shoot down any of them was by diving on them, or by waiting for them over their home base.'

One of the major roles of the 262s was to strafe the masses of Allied transport as it advanced, and also to scatter anti-personnel bombs over Allied airfields in the hope of slowing down the rate of operation of the fighter-bombers. These tactics produced the following advice to members of 122 Wing: 'Personnel are strongly advised to throw dignity to the winds and themselves to the earth immediately they hear unusual whistling noises, or the firing of the local ack-ack. It is better to be laughed at than mourned over. A warning of the approach of hostile aircraft will be given on the Tannoy whenever time permits — that is, whenever the time permits it to be given before the golden voice makes its own getaway.'

Tempest pilots pursued the 262s with all the power at their disposal, occasionally diving on them at speeds which reached a phenomenal (for that time) 545mph, faster than the dive of a jet-powered Vampire fighter after the war. But the 262s were more than a match, as is shown by 122 Wing's total 'kill' of this type which, at the end of the war, stood at only eight destroyed and 15 damaged.

The final days, up to the official cease-fire in western Europe, were spent in an orgy of target practice by the Typhoons and Tempests as the German armies fled, disorganized. With their rockets and cannon blazing, they wreaked havoc among road and rail communications, and to shipping around the coast. Gone were the days when hosts of the old adversaries, the Me 109s and the Fw 190s rose up to meet the fighters. Small formations proved troublesome to the end, but most of the enemy were parked in long rows on the ground, immobilized for lack of fuel and pilots, and the Typhoon and Tempest pilots often flew across them without opposition, raking them with fire. Then, at 8 am on Saturday, May 5, came the order to stop shooting. The angry growl of the engines died away, and the pilots, according to a contemporary report, 'sat back, rather dazed and uncomprehending.'

Front-line conference; on Grimbergen airfield in Belgium not far behind the fighting in October, 1944, Tempest V pilots talk tactics, side-arms worn at the ready. This was a squadron composed entirely of New Zealanders – with the exception of the CO, Squadron Leader J. H. Iremonger (third from right), who came from Gosforth, Cumberland.

Far left: With the retreating Germans leaving the airfields they had occupied in a devastated condition, the local labour force in Holland was frequently called in by the RAF to help make repairs. Here a group lay bricks, assisted by one of the most primitive forms of transport, while a Tempest taxies to dispersal in the background.

Far bottom left: Groundcrew work in the open at Volkel, an advance airfield in Holland in October, 1944, on a batch of the long-range fuel tanks which were specially designed and built for Tempests to give them the capability of probing deep into Germany.

Left: Two Dutch boys, complete with wooden clogs, get a close-up of one of the Tempests which had recently helped to liberate them from the Germans. This picture was taken at Volkel in October, 1944, and Flight Lieutenant Friend is, according to the wartime caption, telling his audience how Tempests helped to counter the flying bomb attacks.

153

Left: As the winter of 1944-45 set in, 2nd Tactical Air Force pilots and ground crews faced terrible weather conditions as they strove to keep Typhoons and Tempests flying from often makeshift airfields. At Volkel in Holland in November, 1944, airmen refuel a Tempest V from jerry cans of fuel carried by hand through thick mud, while engine fitters work in the open behind them.

Top: The wintry conditions in Holland early in 1945 produced their lighter side, as is instanced by this novel form of transport for a group of Tempest V pilots between the mess and dispersal – a makeshift toboggan, pulled by a jeep.

Above: A confident-looking bunch of Tempest pilots from 274 Squadron, 2nd Tactical Air Force, stand by at Quackenbruck, Germany, in between operations against the retreating German armies. Sitting in the deck chair, left is Buck Feldman, an American who served as a fighter pilot with the RAF on Hurricanes, Typhoons and Tempests.

Right: On the flight line at RAF Fassberg, Germany, in 1947, Tempest IIs stand ready armed with rocket projectiles, four under each wing. In the background, the ravages of war on the hangar are slowly being repaired.

Below: A close-up of the four rocket projectiles under the port wing of a Tempest II at Fassberg, Germany, 1947, showing the rails along which the weapons moved on firing. (Below right) Later on, the rails, which were disliked by pilots as they spoiled the aero-dynamics of the wing, were dispensed with, the rockets being slung from simple zero length hooks, as shown in the second picture of the wing of a Tempest VI.

156

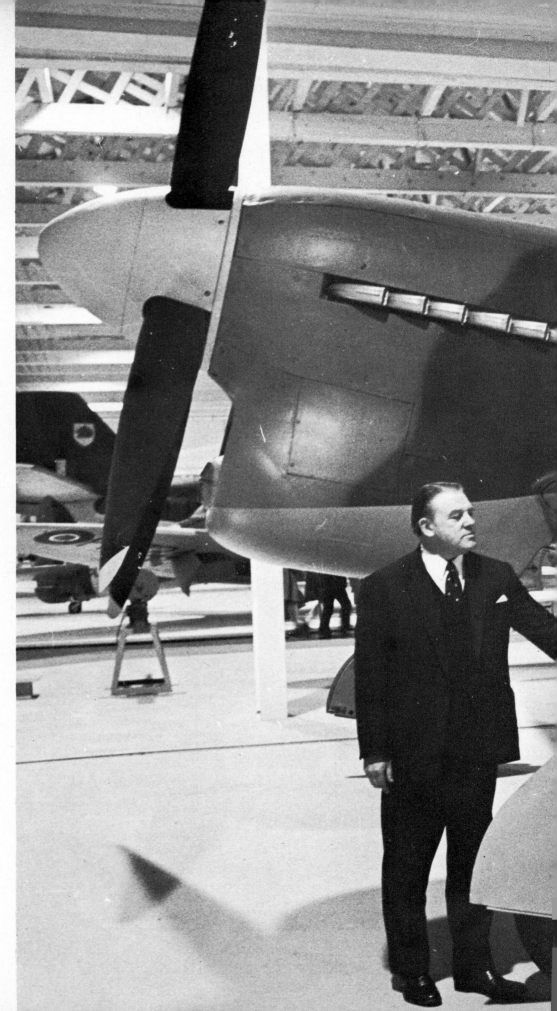

The man and the machine. Thirty years after he helped to develop the Tempest with Hawkers, and then led it into action against the V1 flying bombs and the advance into Europe, Wing Commander Beamont surveys the last remaining aircraft of the type at the RAF Museum, in March, 1973. The picture was taken by a staff photographer of *The Times*, Bill Warhurst.

158

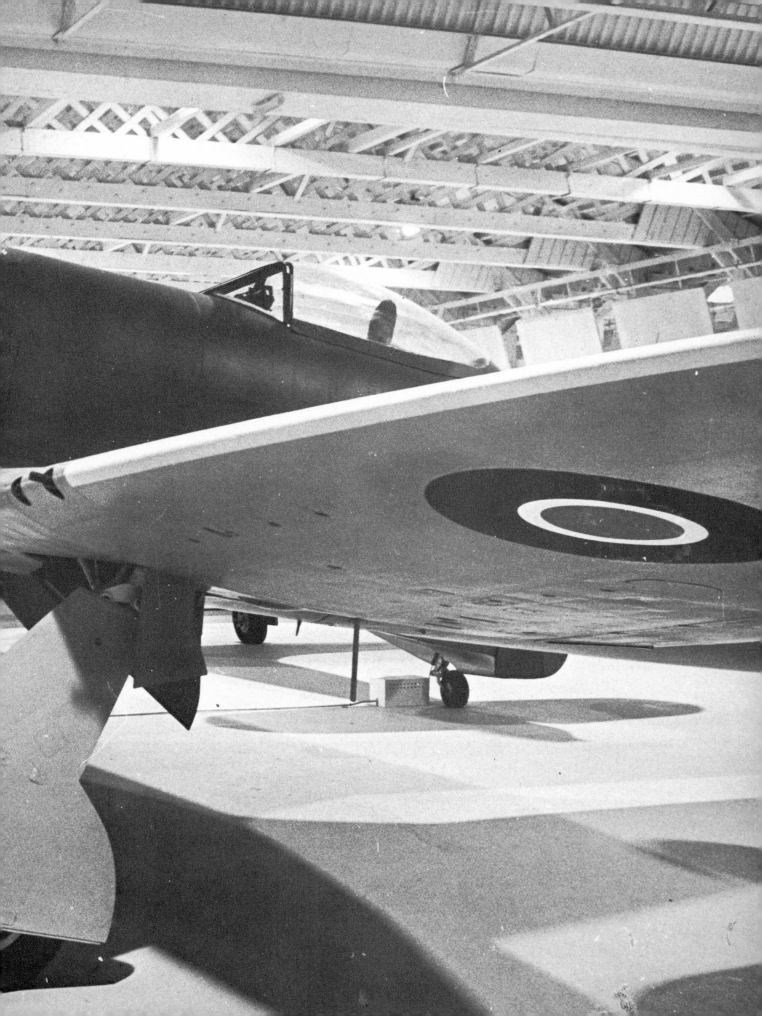

Typhoons in Normandy

Air Chief Marshal Sir Harry Broadhurst who, during the drive into Europe, commanded 20 squadrons of rocket-firing Typhoons in 83 and 84 Groups, 2nd Tactical Air Force, said; 'I suppose that flying one of these aircraft was the most dangerous task the air force has ever asked anybody to do; but from the invasion right through to the end of the war they took on everything they were asked such as VI and V2 sites and coastal defence batteries. It was true to say that against their rockets there was no real protection for armoured vehicles except concealment.

'At Falaise, the whole German army appeared to be escaping until we put in every Typhoon we had in the squadrons. They then simply murdered the retreating army with their rockets.

When the American Army under General Patton broke out from the Cherbourg Peninsula and made their great advance into France, which threatened the whole of the rear of the German Army, their communications were very dangerously stretched and vulnerable at the point of breakout. The

Germans reacted by sending armoured divisions to cut their communications at this point, and this was very nearly achieved. However, the Air Forces received an SOS from the Americans and all the rocket-firing Typhoons were concentrated against the German armour which, in their desperate attempt, had to operate in the open and in full daylight. The results were catastrophic, and many years later this was confirmed by a US army Colonel who had been facing the German armour at that time. He said that the breakdown in German morale was such that they were simply baling out of their tanks and running away without waiting to be hit.

As a result the German attack failed and Patton's breakthrough was completely successful.

This resulted in the withdrawal of the German Army facing the British and Canadian armies, which was turned into a general retreat by the onslaught of the air forces. Again, all the Typhoons were turned on to the retreating army which was virtually destroyed.

In the Ardennes action, during the final winter of the war, the Germans went through the American armies towards Brussels and when the fog lifted we moved in the Typhoons. Once again, there were the Germans uncovered in the open, silhouetted on this occasion against the snow. The messages we got back from the Americans after the Typhoons had done their stuff were laudatory.

Later on, 'experts' tried to prove that the rocket-firing Typhoons were inaccurate and did not knock out many German tanks. However, they failed to take into account the morale effect against the tank crews, to say nothing of the crippling effect of the 'threat' which forced the Germans to move their armour at night, and in daylight operations severely limited their power of manoeuvre. In contrast, the Allied Armies had freedom of manoeuvre and no restriction on deployment either by day or by night.

Nobody likes to be fried in a tank, least of all when they are virtually defenceless against the threat.'

Left: As the Allied armies swept on into Europe, Typhoons continued to wreak havoc to communications. In this attack on a railway line in Normandy, one aircraft can be seen still diving, top right, while smoke trails mark the progress of two rocket projectiles towards the target. In the bottom right corner, an RP has scored a direct hit on the track.

Top: The pilot's view of a low-level rocket attack on German transport moving along a road in Normandy. Salvoes are already bursting on either side of the road, while a further two missiles are on their way, leaving streams of burned cordite in their wake.

Above: A remarkable picture which sums up all the hope of an eventual Allied victory which the intruding Typhoons brought to the people of occupied Europe. A French worker leaves his fields and courts punishment from the Germans to wave to the intruding RAF pilot as he roars over at low level in search of targets of opportunity.

A Brief and Turbulent Career

Right: A post-war use for the Tempest V was as a target tug, and a version is shown here with its underside painted warningly in yellow and black stripes. In the background, a Sea Fury.

Tempest VIs were involved in warlike operations in the Aden Protectorate between April, 1947, and March, 1949, during which time two pilots were killed and another shot down. No 8 Squadron was led by Squadron Leader Frank Jensen who is flying both Tempests in these pictures. (Far right) An unusual close-up of the aircraft in the landing configuration at Khormaksar in October, 1947. (Below right) On operations over the Protectorate a little later. In this picture an all-silver finish has replaced the earlier camouflage. No 8 Squadron went on long sorties below the equator in support of Italian settlers in Somaliland who at that time appeared in grave peril from the local natives they had previously governed.

With the end of hostilities came the virtual end of the Typhoon's brief and turbulent career. A total of 3,317 had been built, largely on the Gloster production line. Last deliveries to the RAF took place as late as November, 1945, but by that time some brand-new machines were being scrapped as soon as they left final assembly. Tempests rapidly replaced them in the operational squadrons, and although a small number were used as target tugs in 1945 and 1946 by the 2nd Tactical Air Force, the type was officially declared obsolescent. By the end of 1946 there were only a few flying examples remaining.

The career of the Tempest of which 1,414 were built 1951, in which year the last ones were superseded by the Hornet after taking part in operations against terrorists in Malaya. These were Tempest IIs with the Bristol Centaurus radial v engine, rated at 2,526hp which finally did away with the pugnacious 'big-chin' outline of the Typhoon lineage. The Tempest V remained in service with the RAF as a target-tower until as late as 1953 in Germany. The Tempest VI, tropicalized version of the Mark V, served as a standard fighter in the Middle East until the arrival in squadron service of Vampires in 1949.

The Tempest II was to have been one of the spearheads of the RAF drive against Japan, following the end of the war in northern Europe. Fifty were being prepared during the summer of 1945 to become part of Tiger Force; but these plans were scrapped when the war in the east suddenly folded, after the dropping of atomic bombs by the Americans on Hiroshima and Nagaski. During 1947, 89 Tempest IIs were supplied by Hawker to equip three squadrons of the Indian Air Force, while in 1948 a further 24 were exported to Pakistan. Both countries operated their Tempests until 1953.

The Typhoon-Tempest story was closed with the development of what was the ultimate in British piston-engined fighters, the Sea Fury. This aircraft had been discussed between Camm and the Air Ministry, as the 'Tempest light fighter', well before the Tempest itself became operational.

Basically, it was a Tempest with reduced wing area, a Centaurus engine, and a greatly improved view over the nose for the pilot to facilitate deck landings. It also incorporated all the lessons learned so painfully during the pre-war and war years through the development of both the Typhoon and Tempest.

The Fury for the RAF did not go into production, although several prototypes flew, including one fitted with a Napier Sabre VII. This gave the aircraft an 'in-line' look, but without the traditional chin bulge, as the radiators were located along the leading-edges of the wings. It was considered the most graceful of the whole line, and was certainly the fastest — at 490mph — of all the piston-engined machines that Hawker ever produced.

Sea Furies entered service with the Royal Navy in 1946, taking part with great success in the Korean war a few years later and remaining with the squadrons until replaced by the Sea Hawk in 1953. The type was also exported to number of foreign navies and air forces. Its useful Service life continued right through to the 1960s, when it was finally retired from duties towing targets. But as late as November, 1970, a Sea Fury won a 1,000-mile pylon race in the United States, and one remaining version still performs at flying displays in Britain at the time of writing.

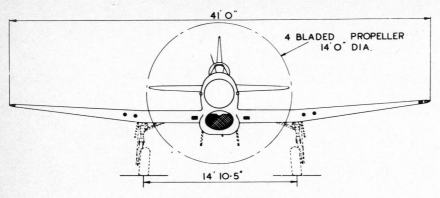

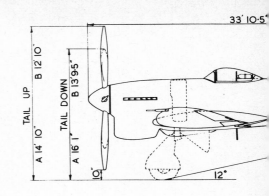

MAIN PLANE

AEROFOIL SECTION — AT ROOT	H. 14/14/37·5
AT TIP	H. 14/10/37·5
CHORD — AT ROOT	9 FT. 0½ IN.
MEAN	7 FT. 4 IN.
INCIDENCE	1° 0′
DIHEDRAL (AEROFOIL DATUM) — INNER	0° 0′
OUTER	5° 30′
AREA — WITH AILERONS AND FLAPS, GROSS	302 SQ. FT.
AILERONS (TOTAL)	24·57 SQ. FT.
FLAPS (TOTAL)	37·86 SQ. FT.

TAIL PLANE

INCIDENCE	-0°30′
AREA — WITH ELEVATORS AND TABS, NET	44·5 SQ. FT.
ELEVATORS WITH TABS, EACH	7·75 SQ. FT.
ELEVATOR TABS, EACH	0·65 SQ. FT.

FIN AND RUDDER

FIN AREA, WITH RUDDER AND TAB	29·36 SQ. FT.
RUDDER, WITH TAB	12·87 SQ. FT.
RUDDER TAB	1·25 SQ. FT.

CONTROL SURFACE SETTINGS & RANGES OF MOVEMENT

AILERONS	UP 15° 30′ DOWN 18° 0′
AILERON DROOP	0 IN. TO ¼ IN.
ELEVATORS	UP 22° DOWN 15°
ELEVATOR TRIMMING TABS	* UP AND DOWN 10° 0′
BACKLASH, TOTAL	† ³⁄₃₂ IN.
FIN OFFSET	NIL
FLAPS	DOWN 80° 0′
RUDDER	PORT & ST'B'D 20°30′
RUDDER TRIMMING TAB	PORT & ST'B'D 11° 0′
BACKLASH, TOTAL	† ³⁄₃₂ IN.
TAIL PLANE	FIXED

A = ONE BLADE VERTICAL

B = BLADES AT 45° TO VERTICAL

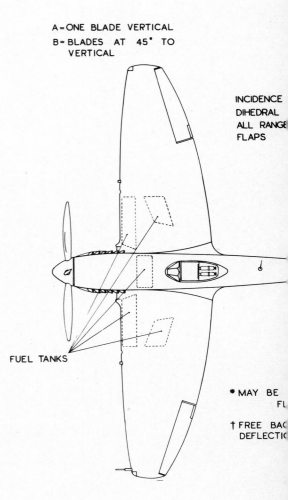

INCIDENCE
DIHEDRAL
ALL RANGE
FLAPS

FUEL TANKS

* MAY BE
FL

† FREE BAC
DEFLECTIO

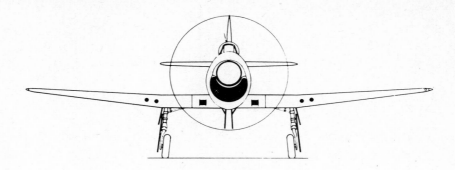

Two Hawkers general arrangement drawings for different versions of the Tempest. (Far left) The Tempest VI, and (left) the Griffon-engined prototype Fury with a six-bladed Rotol contra-propeller.

±10'
±15'
(EPT FLAPS) ± 1°
+ 0°
– 5°

13' 9'

D 8°DOWN FOR
:ASONS

T INCLUDE
STRAINING

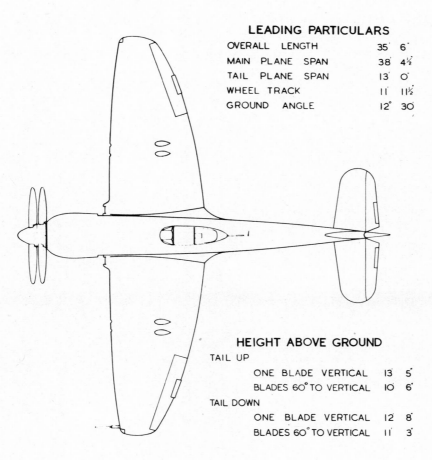

LEADING PARTICULARS

OVERALL LENGTH	35'	6'
MAIN PLANE SPAN	38'	4½'
TAIL PLANE SPAN	13'	0'
WHEEL TRACK	11'	11½'
GROUND ANGLE	12°	30'

HEIGHT ABOVE GROUND

TAIL UP

ONE BLADE VERTICAL	13'	5'
BLADES 60° TO VERTICAL	10'	6'

TAIL DOWN

ONE BLADE VERTICAL	12'	8'
BLADES 60° TO VERTICAL	11'	3'

Above: A classic photograph, taken around 1947, of a Sea Fury in its natural element, flying over units of the fleet with the evening sun dappling the waters below. The bulges on the wings over the ammunition heeds of the four cannon can be plainly seen.

Top right: On the way to take part in the Korean campaign, four Sea Furies fly off of their carrier to pose against the dramatic backdrop of Table Mountain in South Africa.

Right: The Sea Fury went to war during the Korean campaign, and this graphic shot shows aircrewmen of the Royal Navy aircraft carrier *HMS Theseus*, well wrapped up against the snow and sleet grappling, in 1951, with refuelling and other turn-round operations.

Far right: The Sea Fury emerged in 1948 in a two-seat trainer version, of which this is the prototype. The version was supplied to Iraq, Pakistan, Burma, Cuba and West Germany, in addition to the British Fleet Air Arm. An unusual feature was the Hawker-developed periscopic mirror mounted externally on a tripod in front of the instructor's cockpit.

Far left: Deck trials by the Sea Fury on board *Illustrious*. This remarkable Cyril Peckham photograph shows the aircraft a few seconds before it touches down.

Left: Well caught, sir! Deck crew members of *Illustrious* watch closely as the arrester hook of a Sea Fury picks up the gear and pulls the aircraft to a safe stop in the space of a few yards.

Below left: Looking like a praying mantis, with its wings folded, a Sea Fury engaged on deck trials aboard the aircraft carrier *HMS Illustrious* is moved down into the below-deck hangars.

Below: Hawkers had to produce a complicated modification when developing the Sea Fury so that the wings would fold for stowage beneath the flight deck of aircraft carriers.
Top left is the bomb mounting without its fairing, the fastening holes for which can be seen.

Above: A Swiss evaluation team came to Langley in 1946 to test the land version of the Fury for possible purchase by their air force. They are seen here with Hawker test pilots, including Philip Lucas (fifth from left) and Bill Humble (extreme right). The Swiss order was the subject of intense competition between various British aircraft companies, and the contract eventually went to de Havillands for their jet-powered Vampire.

Above right: Civilianized for air racing! One of the few members of this family of aircraft to have been operated out of military colours, this Sea Fury is seen with Canadian registration on a North American airport alongside DC3s, DC4s and Constellations going about their peaceful business.

Right: The Griffon Fury prototype with six-bladed contra-prop.

Photo Credits

The Aeroplane: 41, 110, 111.
Robert D. Archer: 175 (top).
Charles E. Brown: 114 (bottom), 117 (top).
Crown Copyright: 17 (bottom), 20, 22 (top), 35 (top), 62 (top), 69 (top left), 70 (top), 71 (top), 72, 73, 76 (top), 76 (bottom right), 77, 79, 96 (bottom), 115 (bottom), 140, 167 (bottom), 170 (bottom).
Daily Sketch: 84 (top).
Flight International: 45, 50, 67, 70 (bottom), 83, 84 (bottom), 86, 87, 156, 171 (bottom).
Hawker Siddeley Aviation Limited: 8, 9, 30, 106 (top), 108, 114 (top), 115 (top), 116, 120 (all except bottom right), 121, 157 (bottom), 168, 169, 170 (top), 172 (top), 173 (bottom), 176 (bottom).
Imperial War Museum: 49, 85, 94, 95, 96 (top), 97, 98, 99 (middle and bottom), 124, 126, 127 (top), 133, 143, 144, 145, 151, 152, 153, 154, 155 (top), 162.
Model & Allied Publications Ltd: 24, 39, 112.
D. Napier & Sons Ltd: 40, 115 (middle).
Peckham Photographs: 120 (bottom), 172 (bottom), 173 (top).
The Times: 58 (middle), 158.
HMS Vengeance: 171 (top).
The Weekly News: 93.
Westminster Press: 61 (bottom).

Many of the other photographs came from private collections, among them those of the following: Philip Lucas, Frank Ziegler, Derek Wood, John W. R. Taylor, R. P. Beamont, Air Marshal D. Crowley-Milling, Buck Feldman, Group Captain F. W. M. Jensen, D. Helmore and D. Calthrop.